THE TRAINING SHIPS OF LIVERPOOL

Yet often, just before the dawn,
They see in dreams afar
The glimmer of the Crosby Light
And rain across the Bar.

John E.M. Sumner

Now on the eve
On the flood of every tide
How fares the wind for Liverpool now?
We must set yet another course
There's a new dawn breaking.

John Curry

For the Family

Front Cover: *An etching of H.M.S. Conway (ex H.M.S. Nile) by Charles H. Clark by courtesy of John Edge (Conway 1952-3)*

First published 2002 by Countyvise Limited, 14 Appin Road, Birkenhead, Merseyside, CH41 9HH.

Copyright © 2002 R.A. Evans.

The right of R.A. Evans to be identified as the author of this work has been asserted by him in accordance with the Copyright, Design and Patents Act 1988.

British Library Cataloguing in Publication Data.
A catalogue record for this book is available from the British Library.

ISBN 1 901231 31 3

CONTENTS

This book is sponsored by the Mersey Mission to Seafarers, Colonsay House, 20 Crosby Road South, Liverpool L22 1RQ, Telephone: 0151 920 3253

Foreword

By
Len Holder

To people around Merseyside and seafarers all over the world Bob Evans was the padre who did a great job over thirty years for the Mersey Mission to Seamen, looking after the pastoral and spiritual welfare of local and visiting seafarers. Calmly and quietly he inspired others to join him in creating a home from home for them. Bob himself was supported and encouraged by his family, particularly his late wife D'rene who was a lovely lady and is very much missed. The story of his work at Mersey Mission was told in his first book "A Dog Collar in the Docks". The Evans' family journey from the rigours of South Wales to the "fleshpots" of Liverpool was told in his third book "The Way to Liverpool".

Bob is a good listener and a wonderful story-teller and since he retired he has used those talents well. To quote a friend " I read Bob's book on the train and it was as if he were sitting beside me telling the story".

In his second book "Mersey Mariners" he looked back at the history of all the organisations that have provided help and support for mariners in Merseyside and the North West. Bob's research is always wide-ranging, seeking facts in dusty archives, but also stirring the memory of friends and acqaintances who lived through many of the episodes he describes. During his research for "Mersey Mariners" he realised what an important part the training and reformatory ships of Liverpool had played in the lives of so many people - they deserved a special place in the history of their own. The result is this, his fourth book.

In modern and relatively comfortable Britain it is hard to imagine the situation of some young people in the 1800's. Life was really tough, and the great hardships of a floating reformatory were often better than living on the streets of the city. Bob takes us through the streets ashore to meet criminals and ruffians, and aboard the reformatory ships to meet some weak and some very determined young people. He introduces us to the powerful, strict and sometimes compassionate people, who supervised life on board. Most of the "old boys" of the reformatory ships went on to happy, useful and productive lives at sea and ashore.

With regard to the training ships, Bob takes us aboard Indefatigable to meet the young people and the mentors who steered them through a tough and healthy training to useful jobs and satisfying achievement in their later lives. The growing role of a good education was recognised and incorporated into the provision, together with team spirit, confidence and competence that such training engendered.

He also takes us aboard H.M.S.Conway where life for aspiring young (mainly Merchant Navy) officers was quite hard. It certainly bred in them knowledge of seamanship (particularly boatwork), comradeship and discipline. Many went on to serve their country with great distinction in war and peace and they provided part of the "core" of Britain's expertise as a maritime nation.. H.M.S Eaglet achieves to this day the same role with the Royal Naval Reserve.

Training ships in general create a bond of camaraderie amongst their old boys and the Liverpool ships are no exception. Many of them stay in touch throughout their lives and gatherings are always well attended, experiences are shared and the bond of friendship remains. This history also highlights the need, which still continues today, for benefactors, like the Bibby family who came to the rescue with financial support at key points in the history, and for those, like Bob himself who have given service throughout their lives to help seafarers in their hour of need.

The passing of the training ships is regretable, as they produced some fine young people. I hope you enjoy their story!

L A Holder
Former Committee Chairman, Mersey Mission to Seafarers.

Acknowledgements

Research takes a writer by surprise. Often there seems to be no possible means of obtaining further information, but reading a newspaper on film in our excellent Local History Department, studying the house magazines of shipping companies, uncovering personal writings in the homes of friends ... with patience the details emerge. Too often it is impossible to attribute those details to their sources and that is sad. I am immensely grateful to the staff of the Archives in the Maritime Museum here in Liverpool for their patience and understanding. In particular I thank the Liverpool Nautical Research Society for allowing me to reproduce past articles and no member of that Society will argue when I especially acknowledge the contribution and enthusiastic support of the late John Tebay. So many men like him have willingly opened up their archives and with diffidence allowed me to tell their stories. I did start listing their names, but they are numerous and I can only rely upon our friendship in merely thanking them for their generosity. I suggest that their stories will become part of history and that is reward enough even though our names will disappear in time.

Towards the tail end of writing I discovered that the internet included an excellent article on the history of Akbar. Many of its sources were obvious, others were not noted by the author but known to me. In this way we support each other in historical plagiarism and trust that our facts are correct, lest those who come after us will make them so.

Much work is involved in producing a manuscript. I have been inundated with photographs and the selection was extremely difficult. Again all that I can do is express my gratitude for all the help so willingly given. So many photographs and information have come my way that it might have been possible to produce a book on each of the training ships. My family as ever have struggled with my grammar and punctuation ... they are very patient! Captain Len Holder cast a nautical and friendly eye over the writing and I am grateful for his Foreword. John and Jean Emmerson of Countyvise Limited are not only responsible for the printing and publishing, they have given friendship and encouragement. However, any blemishes, mistakes, omissions amd misjudgements are entirely mine ... with apologies.

The writing of this book was exciting and I trust that those who come after will continue the research.

Bob Evans
At the end of the second year of the new millenium.
Liverpool

Introduction

During the middle years of the Nineteenth Century there arose a number of charitable institutions founded by well-disposed people who were distressed by the widening gulf between the more prosperous of the Queen's subjects and the abject poverty of the unfortunate ones whom the bewhiskered Victorian referred to as 'the labouring and pauper classes'. Committees were formed to establish training ships with the object of providing a fair start in life for orphans and boys in poor circumstances. Thus there came into existence the Indefatigable (1864), following the example of the Warspite, which had been in existence since 1756.

The problem of juvenile delinquency is no new one and at that time there were also established the two Liverpool Reform Ships. The Liverpool Juvenile Reformatory Association founded the Akbar in 1855 and the Liverpool committee of the Catholic Reformatory Association certified the Clarence in 1864.

Yet another school of thought, seriously worried about the shortage of trained officers and the general standards of training, led to establishing self-supporting training ships. They proposed to attract the type of boy who wished to take up a sea career and in due time qualify as an officer. The two vessels famous for this task were Conway (1859) and Worcester (1863).

Another training school (not a ship) on Merseyside must be mentioned ... the Navy League Lancashire Sea Training School at Liscard in Withens Lane. This was the first land-based sea school supported by the public and at the end of its time was to be incorporated with Indefatigable. It was founded by Liverpool Shipowners and Merchants in 1902 to train poor boys of good character to be seamen. The Board of Education recognised the school for grant purposes and boys were recruited from all over the country. They were aged 13 to 15 and entered the Royal Navy at fifteen and a half or the Merchant Navy at sixteen. Most pupils stayed for a year and a half.

There was a fourth type of school, the Royal Naval training ships concerned with entrants into the Royal Navy. On Merseyside to this day we have Eaglet.

This book is a brief introduction to the five training ships on the Mersey ... Akbar, Clarence, Indefatigable, Conway, and Eaglet .

THE AKBAR
The Protestant Reformatory Ship

Chapter One

Life Aboard Ship

At the turn of the century, the only means of crossing the Mersey was to board a ferry. You had the choice of venues, Rock Ferry, New Ferry or Eastham. Eastham boasted an hotel with tea-gardens and a dance hall, but the main attraction must have been the group of old warships, moored just south of Rock Ferry Pier. The last remaining warship was to be the Conway, which was removed to the Menai Straits in 1941.

The four warships were independent of each other, but had the same basic aim ... the training of young lads. Conway was the officers' training ship and lay a little south of Rock Ferry Pier. The Akbar, a Protestant reformatory vessel, lay midway between Eastham and Rock Ferry. The next in line was the Indefatigable, an old sailing frigate, housing orphaned sons of seamen and other boys in poor circumstances. The southernmost berth was occupied by the Roman Catholic reformatory ship Clarence.

Akbar and H.M.S. Conway

Far too many youngsters were trained as criminals on the streets of Liverpool. The family background was too often based on 'The Canine Tavern', 'the card-playing beer-house', 'the singing saloon', 'the penny ale-cellar', 'the whisky den' or 'the two-penny lodging house'. The old saying 'vicious parents make vicious children' summed up the plight of thousands of waifs on the streets of Liverpool. It had long been the wish of many benevolent merchants connected with the port that an effort should be made to reclaim some of these juvenile delinquents who infested the streets and swarmed about the docks. It was a national problem recognised by the government. The Liverpool committee formed to tackle the almost insoluble difficulties was called the Liverpool Juvenile Reformatory Association.

The Government's Youthful Offenders' Act of 1854, which recognised law breakers under the age of 16 as a separate group, paved the way for theory to be put into practice. The Act, "For the better care and Reformation of Youthful Offenders in Great Britain", gave the courts authority to send anyone under 16 to a reformatory school at the end of any prison sentence of at least 14 days duration.

The Liverpool Juvenile Reformatory Association was soon proved to be the most go-ahead in the country. The patrons were the Earl of Derby, the Earl of Ellesmere, the Earl of Harrowby and Lord Ravenscroft. It was backed by the Mayor of Liverpool, John Stewart, by one Member of Parliament, by fourteen shipowners and merchants and by the most influental gentlemen of the city. William Rathbone, seconded by T.D. Anderson, in the initial gathering proposed the setting up of the Association. It was proposed that "the boys could expect hard labour, hard fare and a hard bed; treatment must be fair and discipline strict but directed mainly towards deterence. So might moral reformation come through the tempering of punishment. The children would be educated to a reasonable standard, given an industrial training and taught that there was 'A God, a heaven and a hell' ."

This Association started three schools on Merseyside ... the Akbar, on the Mersey, a Farm School for boys at Newton-le-Willows and another Farm School for girls at Toxteth Park.

The Akbar, a 50-gun frigate, came to Liverpool in 1829 and was doing duty in the Sloyne at Rock Ferry as a quarantine hulk. She was moved to the Large Float at Birkenhead for alterations and was fitted out to receive some fifty boys; the first boy came aboard on June 20th, 1855.

The boys wore blue trousers and guernseys and caps for every day, the caps were replaced by glazed hats when they manned the boats, attended church or assembled on deck for the inspection of official visitors or members of the Committee. Each lad was to have a change of linen.

Liverpool Life ran an article in 1857 on the Akbar.
    "On hailing the vessel, a boat was put off immediately, pulled by six boys, in charge of the boatswain. They were clean looking lads; the day being warm, they were lightly clad, and rowed with the utmost regularity. The boatswain was a stout, ruddy-faced tar, evidently from

the south of England, and his sharp-spoken, "Give way, give way, youngsters," met with a hearty response from his boat's crew, and in a few moments we ascended the steps leading to the deck of the Akbar. The place was in excellent order, the deck remarkably clean, and an air of comfort, cheerfulness and contentment was manifested by everyone we saw."

"The vessel is calculated to contain 150 boys, and the number will be gradually increased until it reaches that point. The wisdom of such a step is apparent. When fifty boys are got into 'good trim', have learned their duty, learned to respect their officers, to submit to discipline, which is very strict, and have - which is more important than all, for it involves everything else - learned to control themselves, and stifle or keep under those outbursts of temper which so strongly mark the class from which they spring, then, but not till then, twenty-five more boys may be introduced with some hopes of successful treatment. The staff of officers consists of the superintendent, a schoolmaster, a boatswain, a boatswain's mate, a purser, steward, carpenter, cook, and two seamen, who all reside on board."

"Whilst between decks, we first visit that portion devoted to educational purposes. The boys have three hours instruction from the schoolmaster daily. Some of them in a short time have made great proficiency. The lesson books used are those of the Irish School Society. The master, a mild-spoken, elderly man, takes great delight in his work, and pointed out, with honest pride, the progress that several of the pupils had made under him."

"We pass on now to midships, where the tables are just being let down, and on which the captains of various messes are arranging tin plates for dinner. We descend to the lower deck. Here is the dormitory; the hammocks are all rolled neatly up, and laid in the centre of the floor. By these are bags, marked with large numbers. On inquiry we find that these bags contain the change of clothing for each boy."

Life aboard these old hulks was by today's standards harsh and bleak for lads of poor physique as many of them undoubtedly were. They were accepted from the age of eleven or twelve. The routine was hard. Sometimes they were called to 'lash and stow' their hammocks at 5 a.m. and did not 'turn in' until 8 p.m. Many did not survive the conditions. One of Her Majesty's Inspectors stated "I do not believe that death would reap such a harvest from pneumonia if funds allowed more liberal clothing and more sustaining food". Yet for many of them life ashore would not have been as acceptable as life in the hulks.

John Smart read a paper at a meeting of the Liverpool Nautical Research Society on the 10th December, 1959. It was entitled The Story of the Akbar. Much research was involved and it deserves repetition. Many a 'Liverpool Jack' was to start his seagoing days in the old wooden lock-up, the Akbar.

"Typical products of an age of charity were the reformatory ships, which were founded with the dual purpose of suppressing juvenile crime and of providing discipline and training for those boys who had transgressed against the law as it then stood. The first organisation to undertake this duty on behalf of such boys was the Liverpool Juvenile Reformatory Association."

"During the period 1855 to 1907, when the establishment moved from ship to shore and became known as Heswall Nautical Training School, there were two vessels which bore the name Akbar. The first was originally an East Indiaman built of teak in Bombay in 1800. She was brought into the Royal Navy in the following year as His Majesty's Frigate Cornwallis. Renamed the Akbar in 1810, she came to Liverpool in 1829 and served as a quarantine hulk in the Sloyne until acquired in 1855 by the newly formed Liverpool Juvenile Reformatory Association. Between that year and 1862, when she was broken up, she did duty as a reformatory ship, the first vessel to be so used. During subsequent years a number of similar ventures were undertaken elsewhere and by the 1870's there were in the country no less than fourteen vessels classified as industrial ships, reformatory ships or charity schools."

This first Akbar had served in the Dutch East Indies before coming home to Milford Haven to act as a quarantine ship. When she came to the Mersey to fulfil the same role, she was one of many. There were to be at least ten quarantine vessels in the river off Rock Ferry between 1824 and 1863 ... at one time there were six together. The fear was bubonic plague, cholera, typhus and smallpox. When Captain Clint and four members of the committee first inspected Akbar, they were appalled. The upper deck was rotten and much work was required. The estimated cost was £1,000 - the eventual amount was £2,000. Her condition was never satisfactory and she was described as a hazard! She had only lasted six years before her crumbling timbers saw her towed away to a local breakers yard.

The name Clint is associated with much of the caring activity in Liverpool. He was a remarkable character. He came to Liverpool from South Shields, where he was born in 1786. He spent twenty-four years at sea, beginning as an apprentice and coming ashore as a master. He bought a vessel named Cherub and settled down as a successful shipowner. One of his friends was John Cropper, another well-known Victorian philanthropist. Cropper was an enemy of slavery and a promoter of work amongst unfortunate boys ... and very much behind the Akbar project. Clint became the deputy chairman of the new Shipowners' Association in the port, a member of the pilots' committee, a benefactor of the Northern Hospital and the Sailors' Home, and a pioneer of steam tugs in the river. He also was to join in the Conway project and was the prime mover in launching the Indefatigable. Clint died in 1868.

John Smart continued his paper.

"The second Akbar had a rather uninteresting history. A product of the Royal shipyard at Deptford she was laid down as H.M.S. Hero of seventy-four guns. During building her name was changed to the Wellington and she was launched in 1816. Like so many other vessels built at that time, she never served at sea and for the first thirty-two years after her completion she lay undisturbed in the dockyard. In 1848 she was commissioned for a time as a Depot Ship, Sheerness, then she had a short period as Coast Guard District Ship and finally became Flagship and Guardship at Devonport in 1861. During her forty-five years in the Royal Navy she served four years in commission and forty-one in reserve. In 1862 Captain Saulez of the old Akbar took fifty boys to Plymouth to assist in bringing her around the coast to Liverpool. She arrived in the Mersey on the 5th May in tow of the Liverpool Steam Tug Company's iron paddler Blazer."

"Detention in the Akbar was not intended as a punishment. Those boys who were committed had served short prison sentences for a variety of crimes. The period served on board was intended to inculcate discipline and to provide training in a variety of ways, which would be of advantage in later years. The ages of the boys upon entry varied between twelve and sixteen years. They arrived in many cases ragged, barefooted, underfed little scare-crows and usually spent three years on board. The possibility of committal to the Akbar rather than to a shore school rested not necessarily upon the gravity of the new entry's crime. It depended upon his physical condition and ability to undergo the rigours of life at sea. Despite the protests of successive captain-superintendents, from time to time a number of boys were entered whose poor health was a constant source of anxiety. All too often the neglect and semi-starvation which they had suffered since birth, left them with insufficient strength to resist the ravages of pneumonia and consumption."

In many cases the parents were expected to make a contribution towards the up-keep. It could have been as much as five shillings a week, which was a large amount at that time. The local authority began to finance these reformatories in 1857 and the short-fall was met by the public and the Liverpool Juvenile Reformatory Association. The response was never enthusiastic, but help came in various ways.

The captain in one annual report made a pertinent comment:
"Many thanks to friends for various presents including fruit and vegetables. I would like to remind friends who have gardens, that, much which they throw away, if sent to Akbar would be gratefully received by me and equally gratefully consumed by the boys."

The article in Liverpool Life of 1857 describes a scene from Akbar.
"The boys are frequently sent on shore - sometimes in charge of an

officer, sometimes alone; but no attempt had up to this time been made at an escape. A few days before this, a boy had been sent across to Liverpool, and had to wait at the pier-head a very considerable time, and was thus afforded every opportunity for desertion; but he wisely set a proper value on the industrial training which he was receiving aboard the Akbar, and stood to his colours. What is most to be regretted when the boys are thus sent on shore is not their conduct, but the conduct of those whom they meet, and who in many cases, by coarse jokes and heartless jeers, remind the lads of their position. This never fails to irritate and create feelings of resentment. Yet, notwithstanding this, their behaviour, all things considered, is most exemplary. On Sunday, the boys frequently are sent to the Floating Church, Birkenhead, and their conduct is spoken of by the superintendent in terms of commendation."

Akbar boys

Other remarks in an Annual Report tell the story of life aboard.

"January 11th, 1858 - Try beef at five and a ha'penny a pound: April 1862 - Cook to undertake the barber's work which will save 15 shillings per month: 1863 - Committee understands that new boots can be bought cheap for cash at 5/6d and appear as good as those for which we have paid seven shillings, eight shillings and nine shillings. Try them. Understand that potatoes can be bought for one shilling and ten pence a bushel equal to those for which Hall and Son are paid four shillings and three pence - change supplier."

Keeping the boys occupied could not have been easy. The deck was endlessly scrubbed with stone in summer and in winter. The lads made and repaired their own clothing. As far as possible they found their own entertainment, and by the light of oil lamps they read what books were available. Sing-songs were ever popular and in 1858 Captain Fenwick bought musical instruments with a gift of ten pounds! This developed into a Brass Band and proved to be a popular attraction in Birkenhead.

The Minute books record some grim accidents.

"Thomas whilst employed in blacking a portion of the rigging was accidentally jerked off and thrown down from a height of 16 feet on to the deck, dying three hours later ... Alfred fell from the main top deck and received concussion and partial jaw fracture, was recovering ... Henry lost his finger by carelessly placing his hand between a boat and the ship ... Benjamin fell from the main top, died same day ... William, while manning the working boat, slipped and was crushed between the boat and the ship side. His body was washed up on the shore ... Ebenezer fell from the main top - a height of 60 feet and was taken to hospital where he has progressed favourably."

The boys were always hungry and cold.

"Food was locked away and it was a puzzle in April 1864 as to how Matthew, one of the 203 boys on board, managed to obtain and hungrily wolf down a great deal of porridge. So unaccustomed was his stomach to food in such quantity that the lad collapsed and died! The body was handed over to his mother for burial."

"Meat was an expensive item and there was consternation among the Committee in 1871 when the supplier reported that he was compelled to raise his meat prices from seven and a ha'penny to seven and three farthings!"

By present day standards existence in this grim, old ship was extremely hard. There was little or no comfort on board. The work was hard and the discipline strict, but life was nevertheless far superior to the vagrant existence which many boys had previously experienced. Food was far from plentiful for growing boys living an active open air life. In accordance with the prevailing system as operated in ships of the day, messing was on a 'pound and pint' basis. For breakfast at 7.30 a.m. the boys received a pint of porridge and four ounces of biscuit. Dinner consisted of four ounces of beef, one pint of soup, three ounces of biscuit and twelve ounces of potatoes or four ounces of rice. For supper, dished out at 5.45 p.m. there was a pint of porridge or, on Thursdays and Sundays, a pint of coffee. Tuesday's menu offered pea soup and pork and on Thursdays and Saturdays pudding was substituted for potatoes.

Once a week, summer and winter, the lads faced bath night in the fresh cold water in wooden tanks. Ice would be broken away to ensure total immersion. In 1874, permission was given for an annual fee of £20 to use the Indefatigable's floating bath. Boys were taught to swim and in 1876 of the 190 aboard 134 had learned. However many were lost. It was reported in the minute books: "A gloom was cast over the ship in July by the accidental drowning of two boys while bathing with others from the beach at New Ferry. One had ventured out rather far, and appeared in difficulties when his friend went to help him, but before a boat could reach them they had both disappeared. Their bodies were recovered some days after. The boys and others have placed a neat tablet in St. Peter's Church, Rock Ferry to the memory of their two unfortunate shipmates." There were other hazards from the river. It was reported in 1892 that the tempting mussels near the Rock Ferry slip had caused five cases of enteric fever and one death from typhoid!

The uninspiring diet was criticised by H.M. Inspector in 1875 when he reported that, "The boys are not very robust and there have been three deaths in the year. Salt beef, soup and biscuits comprise too large a part of the dietary. I recommended two or three solid fresh cooked meat diets in the week, and more bread instead of biscuits and a regular supply of potatoes and vegetables." Five years later the boys were being given soft bread twice a week. In 1895, they received a two ounce smear of margarine four times instead of twice a week, and a meat dinner to replace one dinner of bread and cheese. The possibility that they should have milk in their tea and coffee was deferred for further consideration.

An article appeared in the Liverpool Mercury, Thursday 25th December, 1879.
"The well-established fact that 75 percent of the Reformatory children who pass through these places of homely correction and instruction do well in their subsequent career, lifts the good cause entirely out of the region of doubt and despair.

"Considering the strange enigmas of humanity with which they deal - the terrible familiarity with the wickedness and precocity in the criminal spirit - the 75 percent becomes, indeed, one of the greatest facts of our attempt at social reform.

"The downward education of a street arab, in most cases, begins almost in infancy. He inherits the fearful craving for drink bequeathed by a besotted mother or father and, too often, has besides, a natural predisposition for that form of crime which in higher walks of life is called Kleptomania, and which phrenologists account for by an abnormal development of the bump of acquisitiveness.

"Inherited taints of character and an education in squalid poverty and brutal degradation commences with the first dawning of individualism. All the fates appear to be against the child becoming anything else but criminal."

The Inspector reported in 1904; "The boys in the mass look far from well. There are too many puffy pasty faces and skin eruptions. The boys are being dosed with lime juice, but what is wanted is not the means to deal with the trouble when it does arise, but measures to forestall the trouble." Under his watchful eye, the situation gradually improved with the addition of fresh fish twice a week, doses of cod liver oil, vegetables, and in 1914 the feast of bread and scouse dinners! By 1924, the results of the more satisfactory diet were reflected in the quarterly reports showing weight increase of three pounds a lad and a growth in height of half an inch, with the observation that 'the boys are now looking healthy and stout.

Extremes of temperature were felt more severely on board the Akbar than in any of the shore schools. The suffering from the elements in winter was acute, with chilblains, diseases of respiratory organs, consumption, pneumonia and asthma. Colds, influenza and hacking coughs spread like wildfire among both the lads and staff in the cramped confined area, so that infections at times debilitated 50% of those on board. Ventilation on the sleeping deck as late as 1904 was appalling, especially in winter when ports could not be opened as freely as in fine weather. In summer, the boys were berthed midships in a sort of sweat box but even this discomfort was preferable to the horrendous cold of 1894, the year Queen Victoria opened the Manchester Ship Canal. The weather in that winter was so severe that the Canal remained frozen for about 13 weeks, and some of the river as well.

John Smart's article continues.

"Seamanship instruction occupied a considerable portion of their daily life and in summer-time 'Turn out, lash up and stow' was at 5.00 a.m. In winter-time it was two hours later, and all hands turned in at 7.45 p.m. in winter and 8.30 p.m. in summer. When one watch was at school, the other was undergoing instruction in knots, splices, bending and unbending topsails and so on; and the procedure was reversed during the afternoon period. With the exception of uniform caps, all items of clothing were made on board and clothing was washed on Tuesdays and Fridays, in the afternoon in winter and before breakfast in summer. Every Thursday evening all hands were mustered for a bath in tepid water. At 8 o'clock in the forenoon during summer-time one deck was washed daily, except on Sundays, but in the winter each deck was scrubbed only once a week. One wonders if the ship was ever really dry and whether these damp conditions were, at least in part, the cause of so much sickness and the relatively high numbers of deaths which occurred in all similar vessels in the early days."

"To go to sea was a more difficult task than one might perhaps imagine. In the sixties, for instance, it was difficult to obtain berths in British ships. This was in part due to a slump, but also due to a lack of interest on the part of British ship-owners, possibly on account of the history of the candidates. The boys preferred to ship in Scandinavian or German ships, as rates of pay were better, but the Association preferred to find them berths in British ships if at all possible. Service in the Royal Navy was barred to boys from reformatory ships, although in later years a few were accepted as stoker ratings."

"When first opened in 1855 the original Akbar was moored in the Great Float, Birkenhead. But dock works there led to her removal to a berth off Rock Ferry. The other training ships were later arrivals. The Conway arrived in 1859, the Clarence in August 1864 and the Indefatigable in 1864. The situation of these ships, although well up river, was exposed, but it enabled the boys to obtain their full share of practical boat handling in all states of the weather. There are a number of instances upon record of prompt and efficient boat handling being responsible for some very dramatic rescues from the cold waters of the Mersey. For individual acts of rescue the Liverpool Shipwreck and Humane Society medal was awarded on various occasions to Akbar boys."

"Life both within and without the ship was not altogether devoid of excitement from time to time. There was the ever present prospect of one or the other training ships breaking adrift from her moorings. The Akbar herself was in trouble a time or two from this cause, and during a wild January night in 1877 she dragged and ran ashore between Rock Ferry and New Ferry."

"As far as possible the boys were taught trades, and the carpenter and his crew built boats, made spare spars and so on and were responsible for the maintenance of the ship. The ferry undertakings which in the early days were private ventures had always been interested in the Akbar. Messrs. Hetherington and Thwaites of the Rock Ferry Steam Packet Company gave use of their vessels without charge on many occasions. Reciprocally, when in 1866 the seamen of the Rock Ferry paddlers went out on strike, the Akbar boys manned the steamers."

"Friends were invited to visit the ship on any day except Saturday, and the ship's boat met the New Ferry steamer if the master sounded his whistle when passing. In the early days of 1855 the boys had landed from the first Akbar in the Great Float to attend Sunday service in the Mariners' Church, Birkenhead. In later years a resident chaplain was appointed and part of his duties strikes a very modern note, that of attending to the voluminous and increasing correspondence. For the convenience of visitors who wished to attend Divine Service on board, boats left Rock Ferry slip at 10.45 a.m. and 6.15 p.m. on Sundays."

"To discipline and train 200 boys was no easy task and the provision of spare time amusement was quite a big problem. Originally there had been nothing to do after hours. This state of affairs invariably led to a fairly large defaulters' list and by the 1880's efforts were made to organise sporting events. A rather humorous note creeps into a report about this time, when it was decided to raise the pumps from the orlop to the lower deck, so that the pumping parties would be under the eyes of an officer. Evidently sky-larking had been the order of the day. Cricket and football were played in season and a certain amount of amusement was provided on board during the winter months. When first introduced the results were not too promising. With typical good humour Captain Hicks commented that the majority of his lads were quite ignorant of games and preferred to do nothing, for which they evinced much talent."

Sport had not been on the agenda until in 1888 the Government Inspector stated that no Reformatory Ship without a good playing field ashore should be allowed to hold a certificate. A field was rented at a cost of £5 a year for the purpose of football and cricket. Captain Hicks persevered and commented: "As they avail themselves more constantly of the opportunities for exercise on shore, the moral tone of the boys is better now than for some years. We have played several football matches this winter, with fairly good success for sailors!" They were so successful that in 1908 at Macclesfield sports the boys won seven silver medals and one gold medal. But it was not all sunshine! One Saturday evening three lads absconded from a cricket match and were not recovered for a month ... one had reached Exeter!

It is no surprise that there were occasional problems aboard. There were several attempts to set the Akbar on fire. The captain reported in 1877: "A little after 6 a.m. I was awoke by an alarm of fire and immediately slipped on a dressing gown and ran down to the seat of the fire which was in the after hold and in three distinct places. The fire was made up on a lot of odds and ends of rope which we call shakings and which were saturated with tar. Mr Webb and Mr Allen were most energetic at the seat of the fire, the latter almost exhausted and smothered with smoke. Fortunately having fire quarters and stations every night we had the evening before filled wash deck tubs with water, so that being very prompt we had got the fire well under before we got the hoses from the pumps and I think it must have been discovered almost immediately it was lighted. This, of course, was after the boys were up in the morning, they behaved well and there was no sort of panic, but had it happened in the night things might have had a very different result." The lad responsible was sentenced at Chester Assizes to eighteen months imprisonment with hard labour.

Most boys were controllable. They were naturally inclined to defer to persons in authority, but there was ever the problem of the bully boys. An example is what happened aboard on 25th September, 1887. Captain Symons was on leave at that time and the 143 boys on board were in the care of the chief officer, Mr Callender. The first hint of trouble was when several lads suddenly put down their tools and refused to obey orders. The leaders moved swiftly through the ship, enticing others to join them and arm themselves with sticks, belaying pins and pieces of wood. The officers were not equal to the threat and retreated, leaving the lads in charge. The store-room door was smashed and they helped themselves to clothing, before breaking down the Captain's cabin door and stealing amongst other articles, his wife's jewellery. Seventeen of the ringleaders lowered a boat and enjoyed several days of freedom before being recaptured.

One ringleader, Mullin, and another lad received three months hard labour and were not returned to the ship. The newspapers made much of it, critical of the reformers and the system of control. Ten pleaded guilty to mutinous conduct before Mr Justice Day at Liverpool Winter Assizes. They were not given any further punishment as the Judge stated: "the discipine of the Akbar is defective, the staff of officers inadequate, and the whole matter characterises a want of firmness and determination on the part of the staff which, if exhibited at the right time, might easily have quelled the whole disturbance." The Committee were shocked by these comments and wrote to the newspapers outlining the objectives of the instituton.

On return to the ship each boy received 18 cuts of the birch and was placed in solitary confinement in the bowels of the vessel in darkness and with a diet of ship's biscuit and water.

At the 33rd Annual Meeting of the Liverpool Reformatory Association Mr R.S. Blease referred to this mutiny in his Secretary's Report: "It is hoped that good conduct and order will soon be restored. These cases of unruly behaviour arise from the influence and example of the older lads. Being vicious and ill-disposed, their example is injurious to the younger boys. When Reformatory boys prove too much for those in authority, they should be sent to a school of a somewhat more penal character, and more qualified to deal with boys of this order."

The Mersey is no place for small boats as the tide can be swift and treacherous. A desperately sad incident was reported in the March 1884 issue of the 'Reformatory and Refuge Journal' under the heading of 'A Shocking Adventure'.

"A dreadful story of suffering was revealed at an inquest held at Frodsham on the body of a young man named Duckworth, who had come from Blackburn to see his brother, a lad on the reformatory ship, Akbar. At four o'clock, a crew of twelve boys, in the charge of the coxswain, were about to land two officers, the boy Duckworth, and the mail, when they were caught by a sudden gale. After gallantly struggling for an hour and a half, they found themselves gradually carried up the Mersey, past Bromborough and Eastham, on the Cheshire shore. Luckily they were in charge of the stoutest boat on board the Akbar, or they would have been inevitably drowned as the waves repeatedly dashed over, drenching them to the skin.

"No less then 8 out of the 12 available oars were broken in the terrible struggle against wind and tide. To add to their misery the night became pitch dark and the boat was completely at the mercy of the waves. Four hours later the boat was washed close in shore on the desolate Frodsham Marsh, situated between Frodsham and Ellesmere Port. By wading breast high in water they managed to reach the shore in the most exhausted and forlorn condition. They were without a particle of food, and were almost perished with hunger and cold. Under the advice of the officer in charge, all the lads kept close together to live out the night.

"The wind swept across the bleak and desolate marsh with terrific fury, bringing the icy blast of hail, which cut up the lads' hands and faces in a shocking manner. A little later on, Duckworth was found to be missing and despite the shouts and calls, which were unfortunately drowned by the roar of the gale, nothing further was seen of him until daylight broke upon the miserable group. To get off the marsh is impossible at night, it being several thousand acres in extent, and intersected at every hundred yards by wide and deep dykes full of water. There is not a stick or tree upon it, and here for 10 hours through that awful night the poor boys bore the full brunt of the storm.. One by one they succumbed to sleep, and were with difficulty roused by their comrades in misery.

"When day dawned, despite every exertion, four had fallen apparently dying. The chief officer set off to obtain assistance.

Unfortunately, no conveyance could reach the spot, and the helpless, almost lifeless lads, had to be carried a mile and a half to Frodsham, where they were put to bed in the Queen's Head Inn, and every attention was paid to them by the medical men of the town. In the meantime, searchers were looking for Duckworth. He was soon discovered about a quarter of a mile from the spot where the lads had fought out the gale, lying on his side cold and stiff, having perished from exposure. The officer in his evidence told the coroner and jury that they would never forget the agonising experience during the storm all night to which they were exposed, without food or shelter for fourteen hours. The coroner said the fact that any of the boys survived the terrible exposure spoke highly of their stamina, and the treatment they received aboard Akbar. The Jury returned a verdict of death from exposure."

Mr Allen, the instructor involved with the disaster, lost his teeth! The committee granted him a remarkable five guineas for a replacement set.

The old Minute Books have interesting entries.
"March 1867. In consideration of many services rendered to us by the Rock Ferry Company, it has been decided not to press for a claim for damages to the galley when run into by the steamer Bee."
"1886. Captain reported the Great Eastern to be anchored in a dangerous position to the ship Akbar. Owners were warned that they would be held responsible for any damage and the Admiralty informed."
"1887. Offensive smell from the cargo of Locksley Hall, nuisance and source of danger to health of those living on board. Dock Board reports they will do everything to remove cargo with least possible delay."
"1889. Captain reported 'My water closet is 8 years-old and on the side of the ship, and during a storm proves quite dangerous to use."

On January 2nd, 1888 with 146 boys aboard, the Superintendent received a message that serious violence was planned on the next visiting day. The River and Cheshire police were informed. It was noted in the Committee minutes that "the precaution so cowed the boys that no disturbance took place".

Two weeks later, 13 lads absconded into the fog. They became lost and were rescued by a passing ship ... nine were sentenced to prison for three months hard labour and the others were flogged aboard the Akbar.

It had all been too much for Captain Edwin C. Symons, R.N., who decided to resign. His successor, Captain Edward Hicks, R.N., took over command in April 1888 at a salary of £300 a year and £42 and 6s. for rations with his quarters aboard. Gradually he was to restore order and discipline.

H.M.Inspector, Colonel Inglis summed up the situation at the end of the year. "I found officers and boys working together and all going on well. The ship has entirely recovered its old form, and is now under careful, firm and judicious management."

Flareups were quickly doused. In August 1892, the Captain reported a disturbance aboard. "I visited the sleeping deck at about 10 p.m. and was surprised to find a good deal of whistling and insubordinate shouting which the Chief Officer was unable to stop. I was very surprised to hear that it had been going on for over half an hour and that I had not been informed. The moment that I was on the Deck there was most perfect silence, but when I left there was a light noise which ceased the moment I returned and was not repeated during the night.

"The noise resumed at 6.45 a.m. and as I could not fix it on any individual, I at once filed the boys on the upper deck and kept them at 'attention' for two hours and cancelled all leave. The usual routine was then proceeded with and the work done in a willing and orderly manner. At noon, two Petty Officers asked permission to address me on behalf of the boys and reported that the boys promised that if leave was resumed there would be no more noise. I at once assembled the whole of the boys and told them that I would make no terms, that leave would be stopped as long as I thought fit and that I would have order and discipline maintained as well. Privately I took all precautions necessary in case of fire or to defeat force if necessary."

There were other problems to be faced. On November 2nd, 1888, the ship broke adrift in a heavy gale and collided with Conway. Damages were claimed, the moorings had to be repaired and the New Ferry Company sent a bill for 30 shillings for services rendered by S.S. Firefly during the gale.

Health was always a problem In one year six boys were to die and the cause was invariably consumption, pneumonia or pleurisy. Accidents could not be prevented. An inspector in 1893 made this comment. "The one weak point in the ship is her record of sickness. The fact that health on board during the past ten years, as judged by the vital statistics, does not appear to be up to the level of other ships, demands the careful consideration of the Committee." This was the report that resulted in the boys spending a fortnight in the Cholera Hospital in New Ferry, which happily was empty at the time.

The old ship was fumigated and cleaned, new timber was installed to replace the old decaying wood.

The captain reported:
"The result of the experiment was most successful, not only has the condition of the ship been improved but the boys have benefited greatly from the change and the run in the grass field during the magnificent weather. Relaxation of discipline was unavoidable in such a place but the lads could not have behaved better and in no instance did they take advantage of the almost absolute freedom. They returned in the best of health and spirits."

In December 1894, smallpox broke out in Clarence and all the Akbar boys were vaccinated at a cost of one shilling each. Epidemics ashore often left the ship isolated. Staff frequently requested leave 'to recoup my health' and the failing health of others would force them to resign. Back in 1866, the Schoolmaster had moved out for a 'change of air' and in the following year the Bandmaster stated that 'The cold state of the orlop deck forced him to depart before the onset of winter'. Captain Urmston, R.N., died in 1867 of 'congestion of the lungs brought on by typhoid fever'!

Because Akbar was so closely moored to the more influential Conway,it was ideally placed to cream off many of the latter's illustrious visitors. There were visits from the Prince of Wales, the Sultan of Zanzibar, the Duke of Edinburgh and in 1861, Prince Albert was escorted under the guidance of the Mayor and in expressing his 'approbation of the purpose of the Institution' praised the order and cleanliness of all on board, and promised the boys buns and apples. Other honoured guests included the Lords of the Admiralty, the Bishop of Sydney, the Japanese Ambassador, the Earl of Devon, Lords Carnarvon, Derby and Clarendon, the Marquis of Westminster and an American gentleman, the Honourable Mr Pearse, calling on an order from his Secretary of State to see the ship. The thoughts of the boys on the work involved in such visits is not recorded!

In ceremonial rig

The visit of the Duke of Edinburgh on 23rd June, 1896 received wide press coverage.

"It was ten minutes of 12 o'clock when the Duke of Edinburgh re-embarked on board the Alert at Birkenhead Ferry, after leaving the ship building yard of Messrs Laird Bros. At this time the atmosphere was remarkably clear, and a brilliant sunshine imparted great beauty to the scene on the river. Before quitting the Mersey his Royal Highness had determined to pay a visit to the Akbar and Clarence, the Reformatory ships and the training ship, Indefatigable; the Alert steamed up the river, and in passing her Majesty's ship Donegal, a royal salute was fired from the vessel, the band having previously played 'God save the Queen'. Reaching the Akbar, the Prince proceeded on board and was received by Captain Borland, R.N., the Master and members of the Committee.

"On board were 186 boys, the whole of whom had an exceedingly clean and smart appearance. Upon his Royal Highness leaving Akbar, the greater number of boys manned the yards, whilst another party of them sang 'God save the Queen' in beautiful style."

Motivation to encourage good behaviour on board was important. After a year's detention boys of exemplary behaviour were allowed home leave for between 10 and 14 days ... in 1857, 31 country boys were given this privilege. It was noticed that this often produced an improvement in health, conduct and disposition. By 1896, the boys (24 altogether) were being sent on errands ashore to 'test their moral courage and powers of self-control'. In their bright uniforms with shaved heads they were closely observed and the slightest hint of bad manners or misbehaviour was reported by the public.

The Committee members were very selective as to whom they allowed on board Akbar, whether inmates or visitors. There was appalling bigotry in keeping with the thoughts of the time ... today they would have fallen foul of the Race Relations and Civil Liberties campaigners. In June 1856 the Committee received a request for the admission of 'a boy of colour' and it was refused on the grounds that 'the discipline of the ship is at present so imperfect such a boy be not received, but that the committee will be glad to receive any other'.
Visitors were banned in April 1864, 'for having brought vermin aboard'. Former inmates of doubtful character who visited their pals were immediately removed and one notoriously bad lad who had come on board with a friend with evil intent was hosed out of the ship with a 'water cannon'. There was no room either for George, a 13-year old

petty thief who was most anxious to join his brother. Birds of a feather flocking together could cause extra trouble!

Roman Catholics were not generally welcome in the early days. The Committee reluctantly agreed to accept two, but when the Reverend Father Brown, a Birkenhead priest, wrote to the Akbar captain asking to visit the two boys, he received a curt reply from the secretary ... 'As the Act of Parliament left the religious instruction in the hands of the Committee, they respectfully declined Mr Brown's interference'.

By 1863, the increase in the number of applications for the admission of Roman Catholics delinquents was causing concern. The superintendents of all three of the Association's schools were instructed not to receive any more Roman Catholics, until the Committee had taken legal advice. As a result, it was the opinion of the Liverpool Recorder that any claim by a Roman Catholic priest to be admitted on board Akbar with a view to the religious teaching of Roman Catholic boys was out of order. This was confirmed by legal counsel. As far as the lads of Akbar were concerned the teaching was strictly that of the Church of England.

The accommodation problem of Roman Catholic delinquents was resolved in March 1864, when prominent Roman Catholics on Merseyside decided to provide a reformatory ship of their own. She was the Clarence, which took up position a third of a mile off Rock Ferry, alongside Akbar, the Indefatigable (a ship for orphans of seafarers and lads of good character) and H.M.S. Conway, a school frigate for the training of the sons of gentlemen as future officers.

A brave attempt was made to motivate the boys by every means of encouragement. The Lord Mayor of Liverpool was aboard Akbar on the 9th September, 1901 for the distribution of prizes. The categories tell the story. Most of the prizes were books for the improvement of the mind. Excellence in all school subjects; Bible Knowledge; Religious Knowledge; Catechism; Reading; Writing and Dictation; Arithmetic; Geography; History; Mental Arithmetic; Tailoring; Seamanship;

Sailmaking; Swimming; Good and Manly Conduct; Gymnastics. The final subject was an Essay - the senior class, "My duty as an Englishman" and the junior class, "Six useful animals, their homes and habits".

On reflection one wonders how the modern young lad of eleven and twelve would cope with the challenge!

The Hicks family showed much care for the youngsters in their charge. In 1898 Mrs Hicks opened a tuck shop on board and it proved an instant success. The H. M Inspector wrote: "A lad can buy any article from a red herring to a pocket handkerchief for a copper, but as those coppers are not very numerous, the lads appreciate being able to buy their sweets, ginger beer and treats, in many cases for less than wholesale price. It has brought Mrs Hicks into closer contact with boys, as much talking can be done over the sale of an ounce of toffee. It enables the lads to better show their kindly feeling one to another and brings out the better side of their humanity."

Joan Rimmer in her book Yesterday's Naughty Children quotes the newspaper correspondence of a 98-year-old former Akbar lad . He wrote: "I was sent to Akbar at the age of fifteen for stealing and was quickly made aware of the tough discipline. One day I cheeked the officer badly and the Captain, awarding me 15 strokes of the birch, told the man known as the Punishment Corporal -'See that you give this rascal a sound flogging'. Having seen the ship's carpenter making the long whippy rods from supplies of fresh green well-budded birch switches brought aboard every so often, I quaked.

"All the boys paraded on the quarterdeck, where the flogging-horse had been put out. I was stretched across it, with my legs and arms tied with canvas straps so that I couldn't move and my duck pants were pulled down. Then the Corporal, taking his time, birched me on my bare buttocks, swishing me with all the vigour he could muster. I clenched my teeth and tried not to squeal, but at the third stroke I let out an ear-splitting yell. It was like nothing I had ever experienced ... my weals burned and stung like fire and I howled unashamedly.

"When they released me from the horse, my bottom, cut and bleeding all over from the birch strokes, was like a white-hot ball of fire and I stood in front of the ship's company, weeping and squirming with the pain and humiliation.

"After a few weeks my scars disappeared and I was none the worse for being flogged. Indeed, the Akbar taught me self-respect and made a new boy of me. I have only praise for the officers - even the Corporal, who was a kindly man, but with a stern sense of duty.

"Training ships like this are what young hooligans need today. A caning outside the trousers, though unpleasant, didn't worry us too much, but a birching on the bare skin was something we greatly feared - it really hurt."

I suspect that we must make our own judgement on this recollection.

Captain Hicks reported to the Committee in 1900: "Over 2,500 boys have passed through the Akbar since her establishment forty-six years ago and we know from official returns that 23 of these are under detention in prison in 1900. This is less than one per cent. The respectable appearance of the old lads who have visited the ship and who have otherwise been heard of is the best evidence of the success of our work. In the many letters I have received from old boys, kindly reference is made to Akbar. It is a good sign when boys speak well of their old school."

Sadly Captain Hicks fell victim to the living conditions aboard. In summer the heat was like a sweat shop with poor air and high humidity. In winter life was even harder for all on board. Inadequate heating did not help in the bitterly cold damp days with the ever present danger of infection common to all the old wooden walls. In August 1902 the

Captain was given six months leave in an attempt to recuperate his failing health. He was to die within a month.

The funeral reflected the respect of all who knew the man. The ship's bugle corps was present and Captain Stanhope of H.M.S. Eaglet sent a firing party. Mrs Hicks received a cheque for £112 10s in appreciation of her husband's services.

The new commander took over in the November with a cheque to the value of £42 6s for rations on board!

The ravages of time and the effects of long service were becoming increasingly apparent and for years repairs and maintenance had been a constant drain on the resources of the Association.

But the Akbar was very old! In 1906 it was estimated that she was taking in a ton of water every twenty-four hours. Age and weather were taking their toll. Captain Powley thought it unsafe to rig the main sail. A final repair to the ship's side at a cost of £2 10s was attempted, but the water continued to enter the vessel. This was the end.

By 1907, it was considered totally unsafe to risk another winter in her and on the 30th October the majority of officers and boys left her. She was then over ninety years of age, had figured in the Navy List for forty-five years and had served a further forty-five years in the Mersey. She was towed into the West Float on Monday the 2nd December, 1907, sold to Messrs. Thos. W. Ward Ltd., and towed away to Morecambe, where she was beached and taken to pieces.

By 1906, fifty years after the first boys had arrived on board, the total admissions numbered 3,177. Of these 127 died, 87 were transferred, 1,787 sent to sea and 286 to other employment, 381 returned to their families, 33 enlisted into the Forces, 14 emigrated, 61 absconded and 4 were sent to prison, 78 were discharged on account of disease and 25 by special warrant. 312 were under detention in December 1906.

Akbar had broken many hearts and saved many lives. Life had not been easy. The fact that in her last months Messrs Clover, Clayton & Company had recommended the use of Condy's fluid to disinfect the objectionable ooze in the ship's midst suggests the end was not to be delayed. For many of the lads she had been the first home they had known and for them it was the first time that anyone had shown any care or interest in them. Akbar had worked her purpose, but no-one would mourn the passing of the floating reformatories.

Chapter Two

The Heswall Nautical School

The boys moved to new premises in Heswall where they remained until the school was closed by order of the Home Office in February 1956. The site was already the Akbar's holiday camp housed in two long sheds and much work was needed to bring the premises to a standard in Oldfield Lane. The Heswall Nautical School, opened in 1909, was in the mid 1930's to become an approved school.

The school opened with 200 lads aged 16 to 18. They started in the recruits' class; this was followed by a brief spell in the laundry or at work with the gardeners and finally they had to choose between wireless telegraphy, seamanship, band or catering. When finally proficient a boy was placed on the disposal list, from which 50 per cent entered the Merchant Navy. Names were kept on the list until a lad was nineteen and throughout all of the time in the school annual reports were sent to the Home Office.

Perhaps the only relics of the Akbar which remained were her mizzen topmast, stepped in the school grounds, and the decayed jaws of her mizzen boom. During the hundred year existence of the Association almost 8,000 boys had passed through the two ships and the shore school.

With the demolition of the Akbar there passed yet another of that fleet of wooden warships which for so long remained as interesting survivals of the craft of the shipwright and of the outmoded system of juvenile education and training.

The happiest day of the year - the Akbar boys,
led by their band, march smartly to their camp!

Another picture of the Akbar is given by a Benjamin Blower, who in 1878 produced a book entitled 'The Mersey' and in a chapter called 'The Estuary' he added a footnote about the reformatory ship, Akbar.

"Instead of being confined to the cells of a prison, here are 160 lads, of the age of twelve and upwards, undergoing the most close and vigilant supervision. Their habits are watched, their morals guarded, their minds cultivated, and their hands taught the useful trades of tailoring and shoemaking, their bodies well fed and exercised by their being put through all the lessons of a seafaring apprenticeship, climbing masts, hoisting and lowering sails, taking in reefs, etc.; and above all, their souls are cared for, being brought in daily contact with the lessons of God's Holy Word, and taught to sing the praises of Him whose name they had formerly been accustomed to dishonour and blaspheme. 'This is the finest sight I have yet seen,' was my involuntary exclamation as I was present at morning prayers, and saw the occupants of this prison home listening to the Bible read, then kneeling on the deck as prayer was offered, and last of all joining in singing their Maker's praise; the sweet tones of the harmonium accompanying their voices. The day thus begun, the deck was transformed into a school. On one side were three different Bible classes, one of which I was asked to conduct, which I did for a few minutes with the greatest satisfaction, being vastly pleased with the intelligent answers of the pupils. On the other side was one knot of boys making their own clothes, while the cobblers and shoemakers were busy beside them. Standing for a few minutes beside the teacher who was drilling his class, the business was interrupted by a young man who came up, and shaking the master warmly by the hand, said 'Good-bye, Sir, I'm just going off.' A few words of Christian counsel were spoken to him, and then he went round the whole class, shaking hands with each and saying farewell. His time was out, and he had got a berth as ordinary seaman in a ship going to India. In his chest he had a clean comfortable outfit and a Bible."

The Mersey Mission to Seamen was well involved with the Training ships and in 1897 a sub-committee was elected by the Mission to interview candidates for the various chaplaincies.

The idea of training boys to serve at sea goes back at least to 1756, when Sir John Fielding, the famous author and London magistrate, had collected a number of urchins who had been brought before him and had sent them to serve on board H.M.S. Barfleur. He also requested the Marine Society, which had just been established, to take any boys he sent to them and to this day that Society assists lads in nautical schools.

The Marine Society was founded in 1756 by Jonas Hanway, a London-based philanthropist and a member of the Russia Company. The aim was to encourage poor men and boys of good character to join the Royal Navy at the start of the Seven Years War ... Britain and Prussia against France and Austria. By the end of the war in 1763 the Society had recruited 5,451 men and 5,174 boys. It was incorporated by Act of Parliament in 1772 to apprentice poor boys into the Royal Navy and the merchant service; it equipped them with clothing and set out to provide a pre-sea education. The Society commissioned the first pre-sea training ship in the world, the Beatty. On 13 September 1786 the 350 ton sloop took onboard 30 boys. This was the start of the era of pre-sea harbour training ships.

The Mersey Mission's interest in Akbar was underlined in 1889 when the Reverend F.E. Hicks, chaplain in Akbar, was appointed as an honorary chaplain in the Mersey Mission to Seamen. Another chaplain was the Reverend Digby Bliss Kittermaster whose title was 'Superintendent of Shrewsbury School Mission to Boys in Liverpool and Chaplain to Reform Ship Akbar'. His stipend was £100 per annum from the Mersey Mission and £160 from Akbar. He was a powerful character, not afraid to speak when moral conditions were unsatisfactory. On the 3rd January, 1907, he reported to the Mersey Mission's Committee on the conditions aboard Akbar. This led to the retirement of the Captain, the dismissal of the Chief Officer and the temporary withdrawal of himself from the ship. He was congratulated on the stand he had made for the purity, discipline and proper care of the boys. Kittermaster was a remarkable man. He was to become the Archdeacon and Rector of the Pro-Cathedral in Buenos Aires, a Chaplain in the Great War (winning the Military Cross) and then for twenty-four years a Master at Harrow. He ended his days as Chaplain to a Borstal Institution in Rochester.

Another picture of Liverpool emerges from an article in The Porcupine, dated February 12th, 1876. The problem of the homeless orphan boy is discussed, just the kind of lad who found his way to Akbar.

"The Newsboys Home appears to us to be one of these institutions that might admit boys of this kind. We are not quite certain whether the managers confine the lads to selling newspapers only, but we rather think they are allowed to shine boots until the time arrives for them to purchase the evening papers. Boot-shining will be the most profitable, a lad being obliged to work hard to sell four or five dozen papers before he can realise sufficient to clear his day's board and lodging (about 4s.6d. per week). The committee appears to be fully aware of the necessity of giving these lads, at a small charge, a substantial dinner of roast meat and vegetables, with a slice of bread, and a cup of tea to drink with it; and by this means they are helping to lay the foundation for the boy's future health."

"The Shoeblack Society is one of the oldest institutions we have. Probably it is the only one that deals with the lowest class of street-arabs, and trains them to become useful members of society. The cost of living for each boy is about 3s.6d. per week."

"The Children's Friend Society is a home for destitute boys engaged in shops and offices; and as the inmates appear to us to be anything but children, we think the name is a mistake. The working of the home, if we are rightly informed, is quite different to any other, and will be new to many of our readers. As far as we understand it, every youth is obliged to contribute the whole of his weekly earnings, from 5s. to 12s. Out of this the committee keeps 8s.6d. for board and lodging; the remainder, if any, is kept in the bank for clothing and pocket-money. The object, we believe, of the youths working in the home is to fit them for stewards on steamers, etc. The institution does not appear to have any resident superintendent and matron ... averaging forty boys weekly, we think such supervision is absolutely necessary."

The conditions of life in Liverpool were never easy for the strays. The dangers were many. Whilst Akbar was outmoded at the end of her days, the old warship had rescued those in need. Thousands of young boys found a decent way of life and were ever grateful for a second chance. Akbar had succeeded for the majority.

Akbar had certainly been tough and when today we reflect upon the harshness of life in the training ships - and that cannot be questioned - perhaps, at least, aboard the ship the boys were given security and protection from the evils of life on land. The existence at that time of so many reform vessels in the country certainly indicated belief in their value.

THE CLARENCE
The Catholic Reformatory Ship

Chapter Three

Father Nugent and the First Ship

Just below St. George's Hall in St. John's Gardens there is a fine statue of Monsignor James Nugent (1822 - 1905). His hand protects an urchin lad. The inscription talks of an Apostle of Temperance, Protector of the Orphan Child, Consoler of the Prisoner, Reformer of the Criminal, Saviour of Fallen Womanhood, Friend of All in Poverty and Affliction. On one side are the words ... An Eye to the Blind, A Foot to the Lame, the Father of the People; on the other side you find these words ... Speak a Kind Word, Take Them Gently by the Hand, Work is the best Reforming and Elevating Power, Loyalty and Country and God. This beautiful monument was erected by public subscription and was unveiled on the 8th December, 1906 ... it had been an immediate response to Father Nugent's life.

The story of this remarkable man has been well written by Canon Bennett and was published in 1949 by the Liverpool Catholic Children's

Protection Society. Today we talk of the Nugent Care Society working with and for all people of goodwill. Father Nugent played an important part in the story of Liverpool's waterfront. His rallying cry was - Save the Boy!

It is difficult for us to comprehend the plight of ordinary people 150 years ago in Liverpool. Shimmin in a book entitled 'Liverpool Sketches' knew all about the degradation and despair of so many as they fought for mere survival.

" ... there is a beer-house, and in this were carousing a set of ruffians, the like of which could not be excelled. Women, without shoes, and a very few garments on, were their companions; whilst brawny loafers skulked about, and vicious cripples stammered out blasphemy at the door. The street was sloppy and strewed with decaying vegetables, and yet amidst it all, young children tried to gambol about; and old people sat at court-entrances, at windows, or on door-steps, with their elbows resting on their knees, in every state of dirt and disorder. But the blear eyes - the wolfish glance - the tawny skins and stunted forms of youth seen around, indicated the life struggle in which they were engaged, and the result could be clearly seen."

This was the world of Father Nugent.

He was born in 1822 and was ordained into the Catholic ministry in 1846. St. George's Hall had just been built, together with the Royal Infirmary and the William Brown Library and Museum. The real Liverpool was less grand. The Medical Officer of Health, Dr. W.H. Duncan, the first in the country, had just been appointed. Three hundred thousand refugees, all hoping to emigrate to the New World, landed in Liverpool and almost a third stayed in the city. A seventh of the population in Liverpool died in one year in Vauxhall ... 5,845 from the fever and 2,589 from dysentery. Of the twenty-four Catholic priests in the city, ten were to die in the year. All this happened in the first year of Father Nugent's ministry ... 1846.

He joined the staff of St. Nicholas Church, behind the original Adelphi Hotel. In 1849, 5,245 people died of cholera. Father Nugent accepted the challenge and within four years he had founded a Catholic Institute in Hope Street and there he was to remain for a further ten years before his appointment to Walton Prison as Chaplain. That Hope Street Institute was to become a great centre of learning and excellence in Liverpool.

The city was a place of desperation. Children roamed the streets in abject poverty. It was estimated that twenty-three thousand were wandering in dockland. Nugent promptly opened a Ragged School in Spital-fields, between Dale Street and Whitechapel ... a tumbledown house was adapted. Four years later there were thirty-three such establishments! However, regrettably, the children had nowhere to sleep apart from the streets!

A French visitor to Liverpool in 1873 wrote his 'Notes on England' and he included a vivid picture of the children in the streets.

"It is now six o'clock, and we return through the poorer quarter. What a sight! In the vicinity of Leeds Street there are fifteen or twenty streets across which cords are stretched and covered with rags and linen, hung up to dry. Bands of children swarm on every flight of steps, five or six children are clustered on each step, the eldest holding the smallest ... in tatters, they have neither shoes, nor stockings, and they are all shockingly dirty; their faces and hands appearing to be encrusted with dust and soot. Perhaps two hundred children romp and wallow in a single street. On nearer approach one sees one of the mothers and a grown-up sister, with little more covering than their chemises, crouching in the dusky passage. What interiors! ... the smell resembles that of an old rag shop. The ground-floor of nearly every dwelling is a flagged and damp basement ... some of the younger children are still fresh and rosy, but their large blue eyes are painful to behold ... many of their faces are scrofulous, being marked with small sores covered with plaster. As we proceed the crowd is denser. Tall youths seated or half-crouching at the side of the pavement play with black cards. Old, bearded hags come out of the gin-shops; their legs totter; their dull looks and besotted smile are indescribable; it appears as if their features had been slowly eaten away by vitriol. The rags, which they wear, are falling to pieces, displaying their filthy skins ... Rembrandt's beggars were far better off in their picturesque holes. And I have not yet seen the Irish quarters! The Irish abound here; it is supposed they number 100,000; their quarter is the lowest circle of Hell."

This truly was the world of Father Nugent, who was to be Chaplain in Walton Prison for twenty-two years. He said: "There is no more practical school to study mankind than within the walls of a prison." Father Nugent not only understood, he was a man of action. Action was needed!

Rock Ferry stage

In 1854, the stipendiary magistrate, J.S. Mansfield, wrote to Father Nugent stating that he was distressed because so many young people brought up before him could only be sent to a common gaol. He pointed out that the Reformatory Act of 1854 authorised financial help to institutions which accepted children convicted of crime. Father Nugent as a result of this approach from the magistrate, made contact with Cardinal Wiseman who was planning to visit Liverpool.

To the surprise of many Catholics in Liverpool, Cardinal Wiseman suggested a fact-finding visit to Akbar. The Cardinal had opened the first Catholic Reformatory for boys at Hammersmith in 1855. He had come to Liverpool to give a lecture on his work at the Philharmonic Hall, but must have had previous knowledge of the Akbar. A group of interested people, accompanied by the Bishop of Shrewsbury and Father Nugent, were well received aboard. The year was 1858. That visit was to bear fruit, although the first reaction was to send the children to existing reformatories and then claim the financial support available. Experience eventually was to show that Farm Schools and Industrial Reformatories were not as successful as Ship Reformatories.

The first Annual General Meeting of the Liverpool Catholic Reformatory Association was in 1864 and it was no surprise when Father Nugent was asked to be the first president. The decision had already been taken in 1863 to establish a Ship Reformatory in the Sloyne, off New Ferry. The time had come to implement that decision. Father Nugent was asked to make contact with the Lords of the Admiralty.

The Conway, the Akbar, the Indefatigable and the Clarence

The Admiralty was persuaded to loan a suitable man-of-war for the purpose. The warship, Clarence, had been launched in 1827, an 84 gun vessel of 2,279 tons. She had been laid down at Pembroke Dockyard as the gunship Goliath and as she was launched by H.R.H. the Duke of Clarence the vessel was renamed Clarence. She was never commissioned and lay in Devonport until the decision to loan her to Liverpool.

Clarence began her new role in the Mersey on the 15th August, 1864. She had been towed from Devonport to Liverpool and work was started to fit her in Sandon Dock to accommodate some two hundred and fifty boys, but that figure was rarely reached.

Money was an immediate problem. Meetings were held in Preston, Wigan and St. Helens in order to meet the cost of equipping the ship. Fortunately, the Corporation of Liverpool came to the rescue with a grant of £1,500.

Much was to be achieved along the lines of the Akbar. The main purpose was to educate the young lads ... compulsory school attendance was not instituted until the 1870 Education Act. The majority of boys, after completing three years in the Clarence, were to be employed in the Merchant Navy.

The Annual Report of the Liverpool Catholic Reformatory Association made an interesting comment in 1864. "The boys committed to Reformatories were accustomed to the streets of Liverpool from their childhood; they have had their respective avocations, either begging, stealing or trading, and though young, they had lived lives of continued excitement, and Liverpool's busy streets, quays, docks, ships and river are indelibly stamped upon their minds."

The first Commander was Captain Edward Algar, R.N., who supervised the alteration to the vessel in Sandon Dock before she took up her mooring in the river. The boys were instructed in seamanship, carpentry, shoemaking, tailoring, etc., and were taught reading, writing, arithmetic, and geography, whilst their religious instruction and practice was in the hands of a chaplain appointed by the Bishop of Shrewsbury.

The success of Clarence for a long time was quite remarkable.

The Clarence

Canon Bennet in his book on Father Nugent includes a chapter on the reformatory ship, Clarence and expands on the problems faced by the Committee.

"Father Nugent had placed illiteracy as a major cause of crime, and statistics bore this out on the Clarence. Of sixty-six boys admitted in 1867 thirty could not read at all, forty-one could not write, and fifty-one could not cipher, i.e., do sums. True this was before the 1870 Education Act, but in 1885 of forty-nine boys admitted eight could not read, write, or cipher, and twenty-seven only imperfectly.

"Disposal of the boys after three years or so presented little difficulty, as they were nearly all taken into the Merchant Navy (not the Royal Navy) and except in times of depression very many made good. One problem which gave concern to the managers was the ease with which they were robbed of clothes and money when they were paid off. A shore hostel was suggested for their protection, but a welfare officer was appointed as a compromise.

"The Association was always preoccupied about finance, dreading heavy outlay on disasters beyond their control. On one occasion a large steamer just launched collided with the Clarence, but the owners of the steamer met the cost of repairs. In February 1880, the ship broke away from her moorings, and to restore her to her anchorage cost the managers £250. In November of that year a boy set her on fire, but prompt action by both officers and boys averted catastrophe.

"They were not so fortunate in 1884 when a few boys set fire to her on the night of 17th and 18th January. In spite of the efforts of officials of the Dock Board, the Liverpool Corporation, and the owner of the New Ferry, Mr Thompson, she was completely burnt out with all equipment and stores. Happily all those on board were able to get to shore safely, and no lives were lost. Six boys responsible for the fire were sent to the Assizes and sentenced to five years penal servitude."

After a short stay in the Port Sanitary Hospital in Bebington, everyone had to be evacuated again because of a cholera threat. The school moved to a land-based reformatory at Mount St. Bernard.

Father Nugent was to come to the rescue yet again.

Chapter Four

River to Land

Canon Bennet continues his account in his story of the life of Father Nugent.

"Meantime the committee of the Clarence in their quandary turned to Father Nugent to use his good offices once more with the Admiralty for the loan of another ship. The Admiralty insisted that first the insurance money be paid over to them, but the committee had only insured for a sum sufficient to outfit another ship in case of fire. They further made known that the loan of another ship would be dependent upon the committee's ability to insure the hulk against fire, and it was some time before a company could be found to take this risk. By November all difficulties seemed to have been met when the Royal William was made over to the committee to be renamed the Clarence. She was a 120-gun ship launched in 1828.

"At the request of the Admiralty, the Dock Board had removed the wreckage at a cost of £2,734, which was reduced by the sale of the salvage which came to the sum of £1,509. The Admiralty claimed the salvage money, and held up all work on the new Clarence until they got it, so that she did not come into commission until November, 1885."

The new regime, under Lieutenant E.P. Statham, was very strict and in February, 1886, there was a serious mutiny. Thirteen boys were sent to the Assizes.

Canon Bennett gives a vivid picture of the events.

"The previous evening a conspiracy by ten boys to abscond was discovered, so they were locked up for the night. Next morning they refused to obey orders, and were joined by three others. The leader, named Scully, armed himself with a long sharp knife, while the rest picked up belaying pins, broken oars, and pieces of wood. They attacked two senior boys who tried to make them see sense, and various officers. When the officers who lived ashore tried to come aboard efforts were made to upset their boat by crashing down other boats on top of them. The ringleaders were prepared to kill the captain, who was still below decks, so their wrath fell most heavily on Frederick John Potter, head schoolmaster, who received three head wounds from belaying pins and was stabbed by Scully within an inch of his life. At this point the captain, known by the boys as 'Hot Soup', came on the scene, and cowed the mutineers by threatening them with an old pistol, for which in fact he had no ammunition. The disturbance was then quickly put down, and the boys concerned given in charge.

"The incident was given much publicity and caused much heart-searching about the whole reformatory system. The Government sent Henry Rogers, the Reformatory and Industrial Schools Inspector, to investigate the cause of the outbreak."

The result was complete chaos. At the next committee meeting there was a very large gathering and the Bishop was surprised to find that the local Member of Parliament was present, demanding information so that he might press the Government to hold an impartial inquiry into the affairs of the Clarence. The meeting was really out of control and Father Nugent suggested that the M.P., Mr. O'Brien, ought to meet the Committee in private. In the resulting debate the Bishop left the chair and no committee was elected.

The thirteen boys involved were firmly punished. Scully received five years penal servitude, and the rest twelve months hard labour. The Judge expressed great concern about the management of Clarence.

Father Nugent had not been a committee member since 1877 and had been obviously distressed by the whole affair. The Bishop eventually responded some months later by appointing a committee of entirely new members.

For the next thirteen years all continued as normal on board the Clarence. However, the end of the vessel was to be dramatic. Canon Bennett continued the story.

"Captain G.H. Yonge, R.N., followed Captain Statham in 1895. The end came with disastrous finality when she was set ablaze by some of the boys, after weeks of preparation, in the very early hours of 26th July, 1899. All the two hundred and thirty-five boys and staff were got away safely, as well as the Bishop of Shrewsbury, Dr. Allen, who was spending the night on board preparatory to holding a Confirmation service the next morning. By 6 a.m. the ship broke her back and sank. The survivors had nothing but the clothes they stood in."

The minutes of the committee tell the story of the end of Clarence.

10th February, 1896.
Captain Yonge mentioned that two boys ... petty officers ... had recently absconded and another boy had attempted to do so. Also some six boys had attempted to seize the gig with a view to absconding.

30th June, 1896.
The Report of H.M. Inspectors in May 1896 stated that: "She affords

splendid accommodation all decks being 7 feet high and the orlop deck 8 feet high. The ventilation has been improved. Noted that a swimming pool and gymnasium are about to be added.

"The ophthalmic complaint which was a grave danger in May 1895 has by energetic measures been stamped out. There was only one eye case in hospital on the day of inspection. There were two deaths during the year ... one from a fall from aloft and the other from heart disease. Three cases of pneumonia recovered, as also did one from jaundice.

"There is no doubt that the class of boys on board is exceptionally difficult to make much of. In the summer of 1895 two boys received medals from the Liverpool Humane Society for courageously leaping overboard and rescuing a shipmate. Early in 1896 a petty officer displayed similar courage in attempting to arrest an absconding boy by whom he was stabbed. But the outbreak of absconding and the listlessness and lethargy in the school on the occasion of my examination indicate a morale not altogether healthy."

Getting work for the boys on discharge was ever a problem and in February 1897 it had been stated that: 'Eight boys had left being time expired and all but two had got work; four boys had been licenced to go to sea, two had gone to shore work. Two had died from pneumonia, but they had received the sacrament and had every care.'

4th May, 1897.
The Captain reported that of the 28 Catholic boys committed to Reformatories from Liverpool since November, 1896, only four had come to Clarence and the rest to Birkdale. He submitted that a greater proportion must have been suitable for training for sea life. The committee considered the matter, but arrived at no decision or recommendation thereon.

4th October, 1897.
The Captain reported that he had discharged the Cardiff shipping officer who had been appointed tentatively and had proved useless.

7th March, 1898.
Several tenders for the supply of bread to the ship were considered and it was decided to accept that of Messrs. Pope and Son, Rock Ferry: about 1,400 lbs. per week ... 'seconds' ... delivered as required at Rock Ferry at one and one eighth pence per lb. This would save some £30 a year.

26th May, 1899.
The Secretary was directed to send a circular to the various Police and County Magistrate courts who at present did not send boys to the Clarence informing them that there were plenty of vacancies on the Clarence and that the Committee would be willing to receive suitable boys.

A Special Meeting of the Clarence Committee was held in the office of the Secretary on Wednesday the 26th day of July, 1899.
The total destruction of the Clarence Reformatory ship by fire between 1 a.m. and 6 a.m. this morning was reported to the Committee. With much relief the members of the Committee were told that no lives had been lost and no one was injured.

The Secretary reported that all the boys were at present in St. Anne's Schools, Rock Ferry, but that arrangements were being made for their transfer to two houses in Shaw Street, Liverpool where they could remain for a few days until more convenient temporary premises were found for them.

Special Meeting held 28th July, 1899.
It was proposed that Captain Yonge go down to Mount St. Bernard with a view of seeing whether it were possible to place the boys there temporarily.

Special Meeting held 2nd August, 1899.
It was proposed to examine St. David's College, Mold.

The Flintshire Record Office state that "St. David's College was erected by Quarter Sessions in 1870 as the county goal, three-quarters of a mile from the town, off the Mold-Ruthin road. The gaol, which included a tread-mill, is said never to have been more than a third full. The control of prisons passed in 1878 to the Home Office, and it was closed the same year. It was sold in 1881 and passed into the possession of French Jesuit priests who used it as a training school, known as St. David's College." This was to be the home for the boys of the Clarence.

St. David's, Mold

Special Meeting held 4th August, 1899.
It was proposed to have the necessary repairs done to the College in Mold to enable the boys to get in there at once.

Committee held 14th August, 1899.
Captain Yonge stated that several boys had absconded, but had been caught. Work proceeded at Mold. The list of damage done by the boys at 111 and 113 Shaw Street was produced and accepted as the responsibility of the Committee.

Apparently the water supply and toilet provision at Mold was desperate and much work was undertaken. Clothing the boys was an additional problem. The good news was reported in the December meeting that the insurance company was to pay the full amount covered by the policies.

The Chester Chronicle, 6th January, 1900 made interesting reading.
"MORE CLARENCE BOYS IMPRISONED.
A number of the boys who had absconded from the Reformatory School
on Christmas Eve were brought before the magistrates for punishment.
William Coyle received two months' hard labour; William Dudley, aged
16 years, was ordered to undergo six weeks' imprisonment; and the like
sentence was passed on George Spillsbury, aged 15 years, the defendant
having previously broken loose from the school."

"GENERAL INSUBORDINATION.
Wilfred Burlinson and John Ryan, two of the Clarence boys, were
charged with general insubordination and neglect of rules. Dennis
Murphy, teacher at the school, deposed to special instructions being
given as to firearms. On the previous morning at 6.30, the boys were
turned out. The two defendants were in one cell. He went into it and
turned the blanket over, and found the revolvers (produced) under it.
They were each sentenced to three months' imprisonment."

"AN INCITER TO A GENERAL RISING.
Peter Mation, another boy was charged with breach of discipline and
using bad language. Mark Lennard, a shoemaker at the college, stated
that on the previous morning, he was sent for to the tailors' shop and
asked to stop and listen. He heard someone say the officers were armed,
but that they were afraid of firing, and that they would show the officers
they were not afraid of them, and would do the shooting; and disgusting
language was made use of. He was positive it was the defendant's voice
he heard. Captain Yonge said the defendant, who was the bugler, was
among those who had absconded, but did not get away. Ordered to
prison for fourteen days. John Olsen, another runaway, was sentenced
to one month's hard labour."

Committee Meeting 8th January, 1900.
The Captain reported that 35 boys absconded over Christmas. They had
all been caught and seven were prosecuted and received punishment of
imprisonment for up to three months. There was considerable unrest in
the school. He also reported that he had sufficient evidence to convict
three boys of burning Clarence and hoped in a few days to give two of

them into custody.
Report on 30th March, 1900.
Thomas Wheeler, aged 16.
George Spilsbury, aged 15.
John Ryan, aged 16.
Spilsbury and Ryan had absconded on Christmas Day from Mold and Spilsbury received one month and Ryan two months in prison. The fire had been deliberately started in or near the bandroom. All three were committed to the Assizes for trial.

It was reported in the Liverpool Post on 10th May, 1900:
"At the Liverpool Assizes yesterday afternoon, Thomas Wheeler, George Spilsbury and John Ryan who at a previous sitting of the court were each sentenced to six months imprisonment with 25 strokes of the birch were again brought before the court, His Lordship (Mr. Justice Bucknill) said that from circumstances which had come to his knowledge since passing sentence on the prisoners he had reason to believe that their ages were wrongly stated in the calendar. He was now of the opinion that all three lads were beyond the age for birching. Therefore he would revoke the order for birching and impose an additional six months imprisonment on each of the three lads, making the sentence on each 12 months imprisonment."

It was reported on March 1901 that the Under Secretary of State had refused to grant a certificate for the school to continue and in the July of that year the Committee had thoughts of dispersing the boys into other reformatories.

This was the end of the experiment with floating reformatories for the Catholic Reformatory Association. They set about establishing a nautical training school on dry land to be known as St. Aidan's, in Farnworth, Widnes. The title 'nautical' was quickly to disappear.

Canon Bennett adds a charming post-script to his chapter on the Clarence.
"Monsignor Pinnington told me how he hid one of the boys responsible for the fire until he could get him away safely to Canada.

No doubt he compounded a felony, but there were many others beside himself who breathed more freely once the Clarence was at the bottom of the river.

"Father Nugent owed something to the Clarence, for it provided him his finest peroration in his campaign to save the boy. 'If you saw a child fall into the river would you not make some effort to save him?' This is the common instinct of a noble heart. In 1864 I established in Liverpool a Reformatory School Ship where boys under sixteen years of age are instructed to be sailors instead of being sent to prison. Last summer one of the boys fell overboard from the ship into the river. Instantly a cry was raised, 'A boy overboard! A boy overboard! Save the boy!' rang across the waters, from ship to shore, and was re-echoed from the deck of every vessel that lay at anchor. As quick as lightening, one of his companions leaped from a porthole into the dark and angry flood. With dauntless courage he breasts the surging waves, gaining ground at every stroke. Now his companion exhausted sinks, again he rises to the surface. Already he is borne by the flood half a mile down stream. See! See! His strength has gone, his hands are motionless. He sinks again for the third time. His little companions having swarmed upon every part of the ship look on with breathless anxiety, and now their voices are lifted in solemn prayer: 'O God, Save the Boy!' When the noble heroic boy, James Ward, seizes his sinking companion, one joyous shout rends the air: 'He's saved! He's saved!' In the Sacred Name then of the One Redeemer and Father of all, help me save the boy who is perishing on your streets, borne along to destruction by the torrent of neglect, ignorance and crime.

"It seems ungracious to mention that the Commander of the Clarence noticed that this falling overboard and rescuing always occurred in the summer and never in the winter. He threatened to flog the next boy who fell overboard and the boy who rescued him!"

THE
INDEFATIGABLE

Chapter Five

The 'Inde'

The name is a proud one ... there have been five ships bearing it in the Royal Navy. Two of them became schools for the training of boys for the Royal Navy and the Merchant Navy. Some twenty thousand young men were to learn their trade in Indefatigable.

In 1863, a Liverpool seaman and shipowner, Captain John Clint, conceived the idea of providing means of training the sons and orphans of seamen and other boys of good character in the ways of the sea. He was concerned about the poor boys in the city. Clint was an enthusiast. With his friends and the help of the Mayor (Mr. C. Mozley) a public meeting was called in the September and a subscription list opened to produce the required monies.

The first committee decided that boys of all denominations and faiths should be accepted for training, although there should be 'daily readings of the Bible and morning and evening services in the form of the Church of England'.

In 1863 Clint applied to Sir James Graham, First Lord of the Admiralty, assisted by Captain Alfred Ryder, R.N., then a member of a Commission of Enquiry into the state of Navigation Schools, asking for a smart, neat, masted ship-of-war for the Mersey.

The Admiralty agreed to loan Indefatigable, a fifty-gun frigate, built at Devonport and launched in 1848. The shipowner, James J. Bibby, contributed £5,000 to transform her from warship to training ship. This was a vast sum of money and a remarkable gift.

Indefatigable had served off Portugal and in the West Indies. Her last commission was in South African waters. Back home in 1857 she joined the Reserve Fleet in Devonport. It was the time when sailing ships were being converted to engine power and most were to end their days as floating barracks or store hulks. In 1864 Indefatigable came to the Sloyne, off Rock Ferry, and the work started. She was to remain there until she was broken up in Birkenhead in 1914.

Right from the start it was clear that in no way was she to be a reformatory ship, but was to be used for the training of orphans and boys in poor circumstances.

Her main deck became a classroom, a tailor's shop and quarters for the captain and his wife. The first master was Captain Groom assisted by his Chief Officer, Mr. Davis; it was part of the scheme for training boys that there should be a maternal influence and so Mrs. Groom joined her husband on board. Their cabin, its ports decked with plants and flowers, became a familiar and homely sight to passing ships and a haven to which boys could come with the kind of problems on which only a mother could advise.

The 'Inde'

The portholes in the lower deck were enlarged to provide better living conditions for the 200 boys the ship was intended to accommodate. The lower deck also provided classrooms, the lower hold became the practice room for the band and the upper deck was used as a drill space and for a galley and a hospital.

It was a brave sight of wooden-walled ships ... Indefatigable, Conway, Clarence and Akbar. Another famous old ship, the giant Great Eastern, was also moored off Rock Ferry as a show ship. The Great Eastern's compass was removed and housed aboard Indefatigable and used for instruction.

At the end of the first year in 1865, just forty-eight boys had been accommodated, but slowly the numbers grew as money was obtained. The aim was still for 200 lads, although the ship could actually house 300. It was estimated that £20 a year would cover the maintenance, the education and the apprenticeship of each boy.

The first boys to join Indefatigable on the Mersey did so on the 28th August, 1865. Amongst them was Maurice Abrahams. His entry record reads as follows:-

Age, 14 years; Complexion dark; Hair brown; Eyes brown.

Height 4 ft 6 ¾ inches; Weight 77lbs.
Where born: Poulton, Somersetshire.
Last school: Christ Church, Liverpool.
Last employment: Watchmakery.
Father's name: Isaac Abrahams (deserted).
Father's occupation: Pawnbroker.
Mother's name: Ann Abrahams. Character: Good.
Mother's occupation: Housekeeper.
Residence: 45, Clayton Street, Liverpool.
Date of Leaving: 4th October, 1866. Bound Apprentice to Messrs Clint
and Co., for 4 years, and joined ship Ganges for Calcutta. £30. (This
for four years!)
Character on Leaving: Very Good.
Height on Leaving: 4ft 7 ½ inches.
Report after leaving Ship:
  September 12th, 1870, left his first employ, but
  doing very well as Able Seaman.
  1876: Drowned at sea.

Captain John Clint was a prime mover in the establishment of
Indefatigable and, although a successful shipowner, he is on record
stating that the establishment of the training ship was the 'crowning
achievement of my career'.

In 1873 Indefatigable broke her moorings and was badly damaged. The
dock repairs took eight months. No new boys could be accepted.
However, back on station, the work continued with the launch of a
floating bath for the use of the boys who were able to combine sport
with cleanliness. There were 149 boys aboard with the captain, a chief
officer, a carpenter, a cook, two school masters and four seamen
instructors. There was no State aid, but the venture was viable with
voluntary support sufficient to meet expenditure.
The Annual General Meeting in 1875 concerned itself about the needs
of the boys aboard. Mr. Shallcross, a ship-owner, proposed that the lads
should leave Indefatigable and take apprenticeships aboard vessels. Mr.
Bushell, whilst agreeing in principle, thought that it would not be

possible until better wages could be paid. The fact was that boys were placed in vessels when they left Indefatigable, but remained for one voyage only because they could receive better wages elsewhere as ordinary seamen. "While an apprentice boy received perhaps £40 in four years, boys who went out as ordinary seamen found that they could obtain £1 a month, and in about twelve months were able to ship for £2 10s. or £3 a month. Apprentices receiving only £6 or £8 in their second year therefore became dissatisfied, though the committee pointed out to them that probably at the end of five years they would find themselves in a better position than boys who went out at first as ordinary seamen."

A letter was then read to the Meeting.

"My conviction is that some decided action must before long be taken to maintain the standard of our British seamen, otherwise they will most certainly cease to exist. The rapid deterioration in the quality of our sailors I attribute to the following causes:
1. The best of them settled in California and Australia between the years 1849 and 1860.
2. The abandonment of compulsory apprenticeships.
3. The loss of the best of all schools for training seamen ... the coal trade on our east and west coasts ... it being now chiefly carried on by steam in lieu sailing vessels.
4. The increased demand for boys in the iron ship building and boiler yards of the country, which hold out greater inducements to them pecuniarily, than going to sea.
Hence, unless better pay is given to apprentices ... as suggested by Mr. William Inman ... and the system made once more compulsory, I can see but a gloomy future for the efficient manning of our ships."

A report written in 1881 continues this theme. It concerns Messrs. Balfour, Williamson and Co.'s Apprentices' Home which was situated in Duke Street.
"It gives me great satisfaction to be able to state that the number of Apprentices received into the House during the twelve months is far in excess of any year since the opening of the Institution. The total is 621. Compared with the preceding year, 1879, there is an increase of 72.

Compared with 1878 the increase is 184. I think the increase in our numbers is attributable mainly to the fact that the Institution is now much more widely known than it was some years ago.

"I make no apology for directing your attention to a notice of our work which has appeared in the New York Sailor Magazine. In the March number ... there is an article on the subject of the Seamen's Chaplaincy at Honolulu, from the pen of the Reverend S.C. Damon, D.D., the Chaplain. Dr. Damon remarks that in his labours he is constantly coming into contact with British sailors and officers, and, after referring to the Sailor's Rest in Devonport, he says: 'But another Institution for the benefit of British seamen has its head-quarters at 151, Duke Street, Liverpool. With this Home for Apprentices on board merchant British ships, I am well acquainted. When I was in Liverpool, in February 1870, the Institution had just opened. The Founders of this Home laid out their plans in the most generous manner for the improvement of seamen."

This report on the Balfour Home in Duke Street then makes sad reading.

"I regret to state that the list of the apprentices, known at the Home, who have been lost at sea during the twelve months is a very long one. At least 40 lads, who have from time to time visited us, have perished. In one wreck alone, that of the Galatea, three of our boys were lost. The second and third officers of the ship, who also were drowned, had, during their apprenticeship, been inmates of the Home, and the master, Captain John, was a friend of the institution. The loss of this ship so near home, and with so many persons on board intimately associated with us, cast a deep gloom over the house."

There had been some comment that, whilst the Balfour Home had been funded by the generosity of the founder, the Institution had confined itself exclusively to foster the apprentices for the company's ships only. However, the Report of 1878 made it quite clear that it was open to apprentices in the Merchant Service generally and that many other ship-owners had inspected the Home and directed that their boys should be sent to it. In that year 456 boys had been received. The Secretary also thanked the Sailors' Home for the help and co-operation they had been afforded.

Gun Drill

Twenty years after the beginning of the school in Indefatigable, the main theme at the 1885 Annual General Meeting was 'care of the boys'. The Honorary Secretary, Mr. Charles J. Bushell, reported that, in spite of the intensity of the commercial depression, Indefatigable was prospering. Describing the boys, he stated that 79 of the lads aboard had lost both parents, 93 had no fathers, 19 had been deserted and only 31 had fathers living. Sadly the numbers shipped as apprentices had slumped to eleven. Again the problem of training was discussed and pin-pointed by the Mayor in his address. 51 lads became ordinary seamen and 15 of them joined the R.N.R., 8 were sent to sea as stewards, 1 entered the Royal Navy, 13 were sent to occupation on shore. The grand total of boys on board on the 31st December, 1885, was 222. Captain Miller, R.N., thought the vessel was beautifully clean, and the boys seemed healthy and happy, and were neat, tidy and respectable wherever one happened to meet them. This statement was greeted with applause!

The Liverpool Review published an article headed 'Making Men of Them' on January 21st, 1888 and gives a remarkably detailed picture of life aboard at that time.

"I was crossing to the Indefatigable by the mid-day boat from the New Ferry stage. A raw easterly wind was sweeping down the Sloyne, and ever and anon the choppy water splashed over the boat's side as the lads bent vigorously to their work. There were ten of them at the oars - clean, healthy looking, fairly robust, - and seemingly happy as they smiled back to their coxwain's repeated 'give it to her boys.' Presently we passed under the frigate's stern, and I noticed that the cabin windows were adorned by a collection of plants, among them being a number of newly-shooted hyacinths.

"I found that we had 'landed' on the main deck of the old frigate, and my first feeling was one of blank astonishment. I had no conception of her possessing such a magnificent main-deck as that upon which I stood. Its planks were as clean as a laundress' table top. As I afterwards learnt, its length is about 186 feet, and its breadth 54 feet, and over its entire length and breadth disported the major portion of the 226 youths who make up her company. They were enjoying their half hour recreation after dinner. It was play time. They failed to agree as to whether I was one of Her Majesty's Inspectors, a City Councillor, or a visitor.

"At 1.30 work was resumed for the afternoon. Briefly the routine aboard is this. The boys are divided into two watches, the port and the starboard. From 9 a.m. to 12 noon one set are engaged in ordinary school duties, going through a systematic course of reading, spelling, writing, geography, arithmatic, dictation and scripture. The other set are meanwhile pursuing a course of technical instruction at the opposite side of the main-deck, and are divided from the former by a long canvas screen running nearly the length of the deck. The second set of lads are engaged in making clothes, learning to knot and splice, to make hammocks and mats, and when the weather permits are initiated into the practical duties of a sailor's life. In the summer they are accustomed to going aloft, to setting and reefing sails, sending up and down masts and yards, and, generally, are taught as much practical navigation as can be imparted upon a training ship in berth. At 12 o'clock dinner is prepared. By 1 p.m. it has been disposed of and the lads have half an hour liberty. At 1.30 p.m. instruction is resumed and continues until 4 p.m. Much of their time in the evening is devoted to reading and voluntary studies. Navigation being an extra branch of learning is largely studied by them during the evening hours.

H.M.S. Conway, Akbar and Indefatigable (with practice canvas set) about 1900

"In the tailoring class, two of them were soon busily stitching away with sewing machines at serge garments. In the splicing and knotting class, a rope was fixed horizontally about five feet from the floor, around which were looped a number of short lengths of thinner rope by means of which a dozen youngsters were mastering the technicalities of knot, noose, and 'hitch', under the supervision of an ancient mariner. Further forward another dozen were busy manufacturing new hammocks, and still further another set were making rope door-mats. Two ringing machines stood 'amidships.' These were occasionally used by lads, who, as if upon the duty of stewardship intent, suddenly appeared from undiscoverable quarters, and wringing such articles as they bore, as suddenly disappeared.

"On Sundays, service is regularly held upon the main deck. One of the most conspicuous articles upon it is a beautiful Connoisseur organ, which the ship's company would not part with for a gold mine. When the strains of that organ are blended with the voices of the 226 Indefatigable lads ... well! ... I know of Liverpool church choirs of repute which, in comparison, are thrown very far into the background. Stand on New Ferry stage some genial Sunday morning in the Spring, reader, and listen to the music of organ and voices as they float across the water, and say if you do not endorse this opinion.

"Below is the lower or sleeping deck, where in the day time, the only conspicuous feature is vacuity, space, emptiness. The deck is 177 feet long, and in the days when Indefatigable was in commission it housed some 450 of Her Majesty's tars. In the morning the hammocks are unslung and are stowed away out of sight. At night they are slung and the lads turn in, watch being kept on the lower deck under the superintendence of a petty officer.

"The ship is heated throughout by means of steam pipes supplied from a vertical boiler in the kitchen or 'galley' upon the upper deck forward. By means of steam from the same boiler the greater part of the ship's cooking is done, a separate fire range being, however, provided for roasting purposes. The prepared food is placed in vesssels upon the shelves of a cage which descends and ascends by means of a hoist, to the main deck upon which the meals are taken.

"On the upper deck, too, is placed the hospital. This is a roomy and cheerful apartment, for which happily there is no great demand. It had two inmates on the occasion of my visit, neither of whom presented a serious case. The walls were hung with pictures and motto-verses, one of which struck me forcibly. The words were these:

> Guarding the weak, and
> Loving the right,
> Be each British boy
> As a Christian knight.

I thought the words were very simple, very unsentimental, but very anglice, very appropriate.

"Sufficient knowledge is imparted to qualify for a second mate's ticket as far as theoretical navigation is concerned. In accordance, however, with the Board of Trade requirement, it is necessary for a boy to serve four years as a practical seaman before obtaining an officer's certificate."

So ended the rather remarkable article in the Liverpool Review.

It was reported in 1890 that 200 boys off Indefatigable were taken in the armed cruiser Teutonic to witness the Spithead naval review. The Mayor again noted that there was an urgent need in the country for the training of boys in practical seamanship and that the advent of steam had dramatically reduced the apparent need for every ship to carry apprentices. This was a recurrent theme. It was also noted that Captain and Mrs. Groom had retired and that they had been 'presented with an illuminated address and a handsome gong from the Officers, and a silver-plated crumb scoop from the boys.' Captain A. Bremner and his wife assumed command.

The 27th Annual General Meeting was held on the 22nd March, 1892 in Liverpool Town Hall and the Mayor, Mr. James de Bels Adam presided. It was reported that the number of boys aboard at the end of 1890 was 231 and an extra 94 arrived in 1891, making the total compliment of 325. 31 had been sent to sea as apprentices, 30 as ordinary seamen, 14 as cabin boys, 4 into the Royal Navy, 9 to occupation ashore, and 2 had died, leaving on board at the end of 1891, 235. Of this number 111 were fatherless, 11 motherless, and 62 without either father or mother; only 28 had both parents living.

In 1912 an Inspecting Officer of Training Ships confirmed what was already obvious. 'The ship is worn out and unsuitable for further service.'

Chapter Six

The First Steel Training Ship

At the 48th Annual Meeting of the Liverpool Training Ship Indefatigable, held in March 1913, it was stated that negotiations were under way to obtain a new ship and that Phaeton was available. The Captain Superintendent of the Indefatigable had served in Arethusa, and considered her sister, Phaeton, as being in every way suitable for use as a training ship.

The Admiralty was not in a generous mood. The bare hull of H.M.S. Phaeton, thirty years old, was available for £15,000. The Phaeton was a second-class steel cruiser, not on loan this time, but for sale. The sum was considered too high and negotiations were spread over a considerable period. Again the Bibby family came to the rescue, not only buying the vessel but providing the money for the refit. Out of commission, she had been lying in Devonport for some time and after the removal of her engines and boilers, sailed for her new home on 11th

September, 1913, in tow of two tugs generously lent by the Alexandra Towing Company of Liverpool.

T.S. Indefatigable ex H.M.S. Phaeton

Phaeton, built on the Clyde, had been commissioned in 1886 and had served in the Mediterranean and in the Pacific. Fitted with twin screws, she had a speed of 17 knots and had been originally rigged as a three masted barquentine with the black hull and buff funnels characteristic of her time. The bunker capacity of 1,000 tons of coal enabled her to steam for 44 days at an economical speed of 10 knots, approximately 11,000 sea miles, whilst under forced draught she topped 18 knots in her later years. Her armour protection consisted of deck plating extending for 165 feet of her total length and the coal bunkers disposed to port and starboard provided a measure of vertical protection. Although she was a steamship she was also one of the last ships in the Royal Navy to carry sail and occasionally even to use it. She had been paid off in 1903 and had since been used as a parent hulk for destroyers and as a training vessel for stokers.

Towed to the Mersey, she was fitted out at Birkenhead by Messrs. H. and C. Grayson. She had been rigged as a barquentine, but the yards and booms had long gone, together with the engines and boilers. There were two funnels left as reminders of her past. The vessel was renamed Indefatigable, the third of her line and the first steel training ship in commission. For a while both the old and new Indefatigable lay side by side until on Wednesday, 15th January, 1914 the new ship was towed by the tugs Gladstone and Huskinson into the river to take up the moorings recently occupied by the old wooden frigate. The old Indefatigable was broken up in West Float.

At this time another training ship, the smaller brigantine, James J. Bibby, which had been used by the boys for sea training, was requisitioned by the Admiralty and was used as a Q ship, (a decoy vessel) fighting submarines in the North Sea, claiming eventually to have been instrumental in sinking two German U-Boats. The James J. Bibby had been presented to the school by Mr. Frank Bibby in memory of his father. In 1935 this vessel was sold to Italian owners. She was sunk by the R.A.F. during World War Two, and was later salvaged and sold for scrap.

In the much loved magazine, Sea Breezes, Arthur Plumridge wrote two articles about his days in Indefatigable just after the First World War. The Spartan conditions, uninteresting food, control of pocket money and censorship of letters, which he records, have to be judged against the background of the times.

"I arrived at New Ferry, Birkenhead, where a stage hand made the recognised eight bell signal to the ship and a cutter came across and I was on my way. My mother came with me to New Ferry but she was, of course, left at the landing stage. The parting was rather poignant.

"Once on board, I thought, 'Well, here I am for better or worse'. The main deck I thought looked very austere and bare looking but the planked deck was nice and clean; I later found out how this was made so.

"Of inevitable interest to a growing lad is food and therefore away to the galley. It was quite spacious and equipped with a coal-burning range. There were also two enormous cauldrons (possibly originally used for boiling intrusive missionaries in the more backward countries!) but now used in the less drastic operation of making stews and beverages. These cauldrons were heated by steam from the boiler room via a steam jacket.

"This little kingdom was ruled by the cook, one Murphy, (inevitably 'Spud') who furnished the best example of an expressionless face I have ever seen. I never saw his expression change no matter what circumstances. He had two boys to assist in his labours; I often wondered whether they grew up to be as equally dour as their mentor.

"Our meals were taken at bare wooden tables, 10 or 12 of us to a table, all seated on long forms and the practically unvarying menu was as follows.

"Breakfast consisted of a slice of bread some four inches or so square by a fraction over one inch thick which was adorned by a knob of margarine (known to all us boys as 'spottom') stuck in the middle; in cold weather this was impossible to spread. This delicate piece of tempting food was placed on a bare table opposite one's allotted space, by a 'cook of the mess' which exalted chore was undertaken by most of us on a rota basis.

"To assist in the assimilation of the food, we were issued with one of 'Spud's' beverages which we dubbed 'cocoa flush' and which had been prepared in the galley by the dropping of solid slabs of cocoa, unsweetened I may add, into one of the cauldrons I have mentioned, this having been previously filled with boiling water. A couple of tins of milk (we never saw fresh milk) were tipped into the cocoa and water, together with a very meagre quantity of sugar, the mixture then drawn off into 'kettles', utensils similar in shape and size to a large domestic wash bucket (the mop bucket type) prior to being dropped by the hoist to the mess deck, there to be rationed out using basins as balers. These basins were used as drinking vessels too, cups being completely non-existent.

"Dinner for each day except Fridays and Sundays consisted of 'buzz'. 'Spud' Murphy concocted several kinds of 'buzz'. There was 'pea buzz', 'Irish buzz', 'mystery buzz' and another variety which I have forgotten, although at the time, I never thought it would be possible. These 'buzzes' were neither soups nor stews but partook of the characteristics of both and were served in those same basins as was our 'cocoa flush'.

"A small pile of broken ship's biscuits was put beside each basin at table and sometimes these were quite palatable, especially to hungry boys, when a new sack had been opened, but if allowed to go stale, they turned soggy and tastelessly horrible, under which circumstances the ever present sea birds benefited. The biscuits were circular, three inches in diameter and about half an inch thick and bore the name 'Ixion'.

"Dinner on Fridays was usually boiled cod, served on a plate, with the usual biscuits, but on Sundays 'Spud' really triumphed. On this high day we had two slices of roast beef and a couple of boiled potatoes, also on a plate, with 'duff' for 'afters'. This latter 'Murphy Special' was of a dark brown hue, but had the texture of cheddar cheese and contained the occasional lonely currant and raisin. This had to be eaten all the way, but we were all blessed with a good set of grinders. Each portion was about four inches by three and just under an inch thick and was 'served' by being dropped on to the bare table, as we had used the plates for the beef and potatoes. To drink, we had water obtained from a tank on the main deck.

"For tea, we had the usual square of bread - we called it 'tack' but in place of the breakfast margarine, we had a small dollop of jam spooned on to the middle of the piece of 'tack'.

"Sometimes in winter, we had slight addition to the foregoing menu; breakfast, for instance, would be varied by the serving up of a thick porridge known as 'burgoo'. A small quantity of sugar was added in the making but we had no milk. On the whole not a popular dish. Occasionally we would be issued with boiled rice for dinner. This, scantily spotted with raisins, was also not popular.

"Our cutlery, knife, fork and spoon was lodged in a locker with our kit-bag and carried to the mess deck when the bugle summoned us to a meal. Except for the Sunday beef, knife and fork were superfluous and the spoon was the only tool necessary.

"All the time I was in Indefatigable, I never saw eggs, fresh milk, fruit, vegetables (other than potatoes), bacon or anything other than what I have mentioned; there were dried peas and such for the 'mystery buzz', but it remains a great mystery to me how we boys maintained our health and strength on this Spartan diet!

"We did have occasional 'treats' though, for instance if one missed dinner through being adrift in a boat on some exercise or other, we should then find 'Spud', on our return, was ready with a round of 'tack' which he would dip in beef dripping, of which he seemed to have an inexhaustible supply. This delicious piece of fat-soaked bread would be carted off like a dog with a bone, to some secluded corner to be devoured away from covetous eyes.

"One unwelcome chore for us boys was coaling ship. The coal was taken from a lighter moored alongside and this operation came around once a year. All hands would be employed. The coal was raised with the aid of baskets and a block and tackle. This was an unpleasant task as we and everything else got filthy. After the lighter shoved off, all hands would have to clean the ship and themselves. As usual there wasn't an abundance of either soap or hot water and a rather miserable time was had by all.

"The daily supply of coal for the boiler had to be raised from the bunkers twice a day and his chore was allotted to wrong-doers as a form of punishment, but more of this later.

"The ship's complement of boys was divided into two watches and four divisions, first and third in the starboard and second and fourth in the port watch. Each day, Mondays to Fridays, one watch would be on deck learning seamanship and attending to routine duties, while the other would be in school doing normal lessons as in shore schools but in addition navigation in the top classes, so that one week a boy would spend two days in school and three days the following week.

"Punishment would vary from being placed on a coaling party for one, two or three weeks for minor offences, loss of leave, strokes of the cane and what was considered to be the most disgraceful of all - 'canvas'. The unlucky recipient of this had to wear a white canvas jumper for the period of his sentence, so that his shame and disgrace would be apparent to all, much in the manner in which a 'dunce's cap' was once used in schools.

"One particular punishment which to me seemed more fitting for the 18th century was meted out (and probably concocted by) a certain officer whom we all disliked intensely. This ill-disposed man would patrol the lower deck at 9.15 p.m. and would examine hammocks for any faults such as crossed nettles or an untidy rope in which case he would bellow 'Carry your hammock on deck' and at the same time roughly shaking the foot lanyard, whereupon the unfortunate boy, nicely tucked up, would have to leave his warm but short-lived comfort to stand on the main deck carrying his hammock and associated gear on his back, in which cold and draughty position he would remain for an hour.

"Washing clothes was a problem. We used to spread flannel shirts on the washroom floor and with a ration of soap about half the size of a packet of 10 cigarettes and with a bit of luck and hot water, we rubbed away. Afterwards each garment was inspected by an officer and one's name ticked off on a slate.

"Shore excursions for the boys were rare. I think I once went to play football and twice for swimming lessons at the local baths. One of the ship's rules was that a boy was not allowed to go on leave or even ashore, until he had completed three months aboard.

"On completing my training and finally leaving the ship, I was fitted out with quite a huge kitbag full of clothes complete with a suit of oilskins ... and a pair of seaboots tied outside. I was given a Bible by the chaplain (the one with the handlebar moustache had gone and a more likeable Mr. Saunderson had taken his place) and I still have this in my possession.

"I did get some pleasure from being a member of the band when we were able, on rather rare occasions, to make visits to some local functions but really apart from this I must say that I cannot recall any happy times I had aboard the Training Ship Indefatigable."

That was a sad picture, remembered in much detail.

Charles Land has also written at length about his much more happy days in Indefatigable. He joined in 1920 and left in 1923 to sail in the s.s. Minnie de Larrinaga.

"Turning to me , the chief officer said, 'Land, isn't it?' I nodded. Whereupon he barked out, 'You must say , sir, when you answer an officer.' And with this he moved off, bidding me follow him.

"We descended into the after-flats, where his cabin was situated. Drawing up a chair to his desk, he opened a ledger of gigantic proportions, and in it he entered my name and address and also the date of joining the ship. Then turning to a file, produced my indentures to see if they tallied with the information I had given him. Closing the ledger he turned to me and gave me a short lecture. 'You will find the life you have come to is totally different to the life you have led on shore,' he said kindly. 'Bear this in mind. Obey your superior officers and give as little trouble as possible, and apply yourself to your studies, and there's no reason why we shouldn't train you to become an efficient officer.' He finished the short lecture with, 'Should you find yourself at any time in difficulty or trouble - come and see me, and I will do my best to help you out.' I appreciated this last bit, for though he possessed a formidable appearance and somewhat abrupt manner, his bark was worse than his bite. Then, pressing a bell, he summoned one of the boys and told him to show me the ropes, and make me generally acquainted with the ship. This apprentice was aptly named Beam, and he afterwards became my bunser (pal). I was to be measured for my uniform next day. Until so-adorned, I could not consider myself a fully-fledged member of the ship's company. This is the mode of life I was to lead during the next three years.

"To the strains of the bugle, I awoke next morning and slowly crept out of my hammock. With clumsy fingers I managed to lash it up, and stow it, then descended into the bowels of the ship to shiveringly perform my ablutions. This being done - and having had my breakfast - I was summoned to the Captain's quarters, which occupied the whole of the aft part of the ship at main deck level. He used the poop as his promenade deck.. In I went to that awesome presence. It proved to be no ordeal, but just a pleasant chat. I was gazetted to the fourth division and at last I was a fully-fledged member of the ship's company.

"I soon dropped into the ship's routine, and everything went smoothly. Came Saturday morning and I was told off to join a party that had to clean the main and upper decks. This was the routine. Shoes and socks were discarded, and trousers rolled above the knees. We were supplied with a long-handled deck scrubber apiece. Led by an officer, we all trooped to the upper deck. The officer wore thigh-boots, and wielding an hose, he commenced to wet the deck while a line of us trailed behind him and scrubbed with right-good will. Perchance he took his eyes off us, and we all started to scrounge, using the scrubber as a prop and gazing soulfully into space. His attention being drawn to our slacking, he turned the hose on us, but being salt-water it soon dried off. The decks were soon cleaned, and after dinner we got ready to go ashore and play soccer. Usually one of the divisions played the other.

"On Sunday the routine differed somewhat. Instead of rising at six, we had an extra half hour. Discipline was relaxed on the Sabbath, and we were not slow to take advantage of this.

"'Rise and shine. Show a leg there, the sun's scorching your eyes out,' roared Jimmy Unwin, the officer on watch. Should some slothful miscreant pull the blankets over his head in vain endeavour to snatch a few extra minutes, the bed-clothes were ripped off him and his hammock was let down with a bump, but it was all very good-humoured.

"Everything had to be made spick and span for the Captain's tour of inspection, and woe-betide the officer who accompanied him if Henry's (the captain) eagle-eye alighted on the slightest particle of dust. He'd receive the sharp end of Henry's tongue and he could be very sarcastic. Henry was the captain's nick-name, as each member of the ship's staff appears on the stage he will be introduced by his nick-name. Ruling supreme came Henry. His birth certificate endorsed Henry Butterworth. Henry was a bit on the short side, but carried himself like a ramrod. His jaw was like the Rock of Gibraltar, but he could be classed as a good old stick. Henry took the senior boys in 'navigay' (navigation), and made them tremble with the aweful sounds of Longitude by Chronometer and Equation of Time. His wife lived on board too, and mostly acted as his secretary. Second in command was 'The Flamer', Mr. Pattern. He got this name by frequently using the adjective 'Flame it', if everything was not going to plan. But 'The Flamer' was quite decent in his own grim way. The most popular officer on the ship was 'Joe Richie', Mr. Joseph Richardson. Next came 'Dennie', Mr Dennier, the ship's tailor. Running 'Joe Richie' a close second in popularity was Paddy Grant, unkindly called 'Fender Belly' on account of his outsize girth, but the term was used affectionately. Paddy was in charge of the sick bay, and well versed in the arts of quackdom. Pay special attention to this gentleman, Mr. Ellis - 'Little Dick' for short, - he stood five feet nothing in his stocking-feet. Anyone would tell you, 'He had a beady eye, and a large red nose, and was always cracking jokes, but cross him in anything and he's as hard as flint!' Leading my own division was Jimmy Unwin, expert in Morse and semaphore. He was blue-jowled and of a nervy disposition, but a decent sort. 'Tubby' the electrician was fat and short-tempered, whilst 'Chippy', the carpenter, was long and cadaverous. 'Spud' Murphy, the cook, was famous for his Irish stew, and his immaculate white apron. Mr. Williams was the bandmaster, 'Bandy' for short.

" 'Joe Richie', being well-versed in the arts of physical culture, took us for P.T. Standing six-foot tall, he weighed a generous 18 stone. A somewhat podgie, good-looking face was enhanced by a perpetual smile. Full of bonhomie, the boys adored him. I kept in touch with him for a few years after I left Indefatigable and was pleased to hear he was eventually made chief officer when 'The Flamer' retired, a position he well deserved.

"Whittam, the headmaster, used to run a tuckshop. His counter was a grand piano. One could buy chocolate and most of the popular brands of sweets, only for cash, there was no credit or free gifts where Whittam was concerned. His prices were the same as the average sweet shop, and he made enough to keep himself in pipe tobacco. Whittam was so stingy!

"Paddy Grant formed a minstrel troupe; he was a self-taught musician, and could play both the piano and banjo excellently. I was roped in to perform. My voice was in the process of breaking, and it wobbled between a screeching treble and a scraping basso-profundo ... not so musical, I'm afraid. There were seven of us, and we practised in the schoolroom. Five had to do a solo turn, the remaining two, being humorous, were cornermen. I gave a song and then broke into what was to be an exhibition of the horn-pipe. It was an exhibition alright, but not the way I intended it to be. I put so much energy and enthusiasm into it that I got my feet all tangled up and fell to the deck in an ungainly heap, and nearly broke my neck in the process. The concert party was a roaring success, and we were all invited to dine with the skipper, a singular honour, indeed.

"Every Sunday evening, scouts were told off to perform different fatigues during the week. For this a small remuneration would be paid, ranging from sixpence to a shilling. Thus, one boy had to look after the lamp locker; another boy would do duty on the ship's gangway; a cutter's and galley crew would be told off for the week. The galley was a five-oared boat used exclusively by Henry the skipper, when he went ashore to his club in Liverpool. It had to be kept as clean as a new pin, and God help the cox'n if so much as a smudge of dirt sullied the white paint. The first time I was selected for cutter's crew was a momentous one. Acting as bow, I made a maiden passage to New Ferry. As we came alongside my oar fouled the stage, and the blade snapped like a piece of cardboard. I was a passenger during the return journey, and on boarding, received three of the best for my carelessness, and was unable to sit down for the rest of the day.

"All petty officers were exempt from fatigues, but were put in charge of a party and made responsible for the tasks being performed properly. One act of a P.O., named Jess New, deserves mentioning. Seeing one of the boys overbalance and fall into the swiftly-moving ebb tide, he made a spectacular dive from the upper deck, and with powerful strokes overtook the unfortunate youth, who began to struggle. Hitting him smartly on the point of the jaw to quieten him, he kept him afloat until the cutter picked them up. In recognition of his deed he received a gold medal with his name and the act of bravery inscribed upon it.

"The night watchman, who was there when I first joined the Indefatigable was an old shellback. He used to spend the night talking and muttering to himself. If you tried to enter into a conversation with him he would take umbrage and chase you round the deck waving a belaying-pin. We used to call him 'Bungalow' because, obviously, he had nothing upstairs!

"There occurred two hullabaloos during the term preceeding Christmas. William, Duke of Clarence, who's effigy adorned the poop-head, was the cause of all the trouble. At night when we retired he was O.K. But when we awoke next morning someone had tarred and feathered the poor old-son-of-a-gun! One eye had escaped, and leered his displeasure, the rest of him was sheer nightmare. To make matters worse it was Trafalgar Day, and we were due for an admiralty inspection. With superhuman energy, 'The Flamer' set some of the boys to work to clean and repaint the figurehead. His toilet was completed in record time, and the business of tracking down the miscreants commenced, but the wily malefactors were of the super class, and not a scrap of evidence could be discovered to convict anybody. Henry nearly went off his nut and threatened dire punishment to the culprits should they be found. However, the officers were baffled and Scotland Yard was not called in, and the fuss gradually died down.

"No less person than the admiral himself was the next victim! After inspecting the ship's company he descended into the bowels of the ship. In order to get there he had to negotiate a companionway with iron tips. Some bright genius greased the tips and when Henry led the way, the admiral followed, at a much quicker pace and in a most undignified position, on his backside. Careering down at an alarming pace, with his sword rattling on the tips like an old tin can, and overtaking Henry, he cannoned into the latter's stern and brought him to earth.. Picking themselves up, they beat a hasty retreat schoolroomwards, mumbling the while, 'Sorry, I slipped.' Oh joy of joys, neither of them suspected that their downfall had been caused with deliberate intent, but 'The Flamer' did. No one could be found to put the blame on, resulting in the whole ship's company being punished. All week-end leave was stopped!

"Every so often we paraded through the streets of Liverpool. Headed by Henry, all togged up in his best uniform, plus his sword dangling by his side, we kept pace to the sound of the drum, nearly jumping out of our skins when the band blared forth in discord. Shortly before Christmas the whole ship's company went on one of these frolics. I managed to get out of it as I was cox'n of the cutter. About two in the afternoon 'The Flamer' told me to take the cutter to bring some stores off from New Ferry. We made a quick passage and got the stores on board. Just then, two girls whom I knew came off the ferry boat. I hailed them, and we commenced to converse. Time flies, and glancing at my watch I saw to my consternation it was three-thirty. I hastily took leave of the girls and descended into the cutter. I was greeted with scowls, the poor devils had been sitting there for an hour. 'Let go forrard, back port, give way starboard, round she goes, now then fours, put your back into it and no slacking.' So the return journey commenced. We got clear of the stage, but that was about all. A tremendous ebb tide was running, and for about ten minutes we could make no headway. I put the tiller hard over and sent the cutter further inshore, but it was no use, we lost way and began to drift astern. I tried my best to infuse fresh energy into the crew - but they were dog-tired, and we had now drifted a good mile down the river. Noticing a buoy belonging to one of the fishing smacks - I steered the cutter towards it - warning bows to get his boat-hook ready. We grated alongside the buoy, and oars were shipped, and willing hands hung on. Determined to stay there until the tide slackened, I ordered the painter to be made fast. It was three hours before the ebb exhausted itself, and practically half past-seven when we got on board. 'The Flamer' played merry England. I tried to make the excuse of being held up by the ebb flow, but he would have none of it, and literally snarled, 'If you had not dawdled on the stage you could have returned before the ebb commenced.' He told me to report to him immediately I had had my tea. The least I expected was to be disrated. Imagine my astonishment when all he said was, 'Oh, it's alright, Land, carry on.' At the time I was puzzled at what he said, but afterwards found out that he had just become a grandfather on that particular day, and he was as chuffed as a dog with two tails.

"Three years had elapsed since I had joined the Indefatigable, and I began to think it was time to look around for a shipping company to serve my apprenticeship at sea. The opportunity arrived unexpectedly.

One evening 'The Flamer' called me to his cabin. 'Get ready to leave the ship first thing in the morning, Land', he said. 'A wire has come through from Larrinaga's, they have a berth for you on the Minnie de Larrinaga and they want you to call at their office tomorrow'. Next morning I shook hands with all the officers, and a great many of my shipmates. It was rather a sad occasion leaving many friends, having always been a good mixer, many of them were as close or perhaps even closer to me than brothers. I had to see Henry before I left, and walked into his quarters. How different it was to when I had joined Indefatigable, then it was in fear and trembling I had approached the feet of the master. He laid down his pen and told me to be seated. He handed me a reference which he had just completed. 'Just a testimony as to your character,' he remarked. 'Personally, I think you will become a good officer.' I had the singular honour of travelling in the galley with Henry, and taking the tiller for the journey to New Ferry. There we boarded the ferry-boat for Liverpool. One to go to his Club, to browse over a copy of the Times. He was in the autumn of his years, and life had nothing new for him. Myself, in the first full of springtide of youth, with adventure ahead, and opportunity racing to meet me!"

"We got a tin of biscuits for painting Conway!"

Charles Land was a perfect example of a young man who thrived on hisIndefatigable years and made good in his career. They had been for him happy and formative years. For others life had been cruel from the start, a battle for survival on the streets, but even for them Indefatigable proved to be a lifeline and equally formative for their future. Boys became men.

It was a happy chance in 1996 that I met an old seafarer who told me of his time as a boy in Indefatigable ... his name was Billy Maclean. Billy was born in 1911 and when I met him he was 85, living alone in a spotless flat and he was obviously delighted to find someone interested in his past.

"I first came across Indefatigable when with two mates I called in the office in Victoria Street - on the glass door it said Training Ship Indefatigable. The man talked to us. 'Are you hungry?' There was only one answer to that. 'Do you want a wash?' I explained that we went into the park and always had a wash every day in the lake. 'Where do you sleep?' At that time we had found an old church and that was fine for us. I must have been about ten at that time and there was nothing at home. We lived in a hovel, my Mam and four children. It wasn't much and we ate what we could find. My Dad was long gone! The best place was Great Homer Street Market. If you helped with hand-carts, you got an apple. Everyone I knew was poor!"

Details were taken in the office and Billy thought that nothing more would happen because he was too young. His life of fighting for survival on the streets of Liverpool continued in the same old way ... but he had not been forgotten.

That chaplain who had spoken to Billy made contact with his mother and on the 5th November, 1925, the indentures were signed by the Commander of Indefatigable, by Billy and by Elizabeth Maclean, his mother. Billy was thirteen and a half years old. He continued with his tale as we sipped our coffee.

"There seemed to be about three hundred lads aboard. Along with the other new boys, I stripped naked and washed myself in half a barrel of cold water and carbolic soap. I had my own tooth-brush and was given powder on a piece of paper ... it was great to clean my teeth! We sat at tables, six lads on either side with a top boy with a cane at the end. I'd never come across Grace at meals before, but I remember it now.

We present at the table, Lord,
Let manna to our souls be given,
From bread sent down from heaven.

We all gave a loud Amen and sat down. The food was horrible; I shut my eyes to eat it, but I was always hungry.

"The bugle went at six. We slept in hammocks which were great; tucked in the hammock was the only private place aboard the ship. I felt safe in mine. The light was very poor in the ship and because we were for ever scrubbing, it was always damp. But we lads were healthy, so it must have been all right. It was a sad-faced place, but we were fed, safe and warm. Remember we were just street urchins.

"They tried to make us seamen, but I don't think it worked. I did learn how to splice. After three months I was allowed to go home to see my mother for two hours and then had to report back to Rock Ferry. We rang the large bell and the cutter came to get us. We all learned how to pull an oar; that was the only fun that I can remember.

"The Chaplain was a good man. He talked to us and opened all our parcels and divided any food amongst us all. Punishment was three or six cuts over the vaulting horse with a half inch cane ... most of it was for nothing much! Into our hammocks at seven and emergency lights only.

"Never saw the Captain or his wife or his dog. We never troubled each other! We were just a bunch of strays. Another punishment was to stand under the clock with your hammock on your shoulders for two hours. That was hard. I was sent there and told 'You're leaving!' I jumped into the tub, then received my kit and was told to join Bibby's Leicestershire as a bridge boy. There was no time to go home to tell my mother or wish her good-bye.

"I spent two years in the Indefatigable and thirty years at sea. It did me no harm and did teach me to respect God."

Billy was a quiet, courteous gentleman. Like so many old seafarers, he knew that most people were not in the least interested in his years at sea and, even if they were, did not know how to ask the right questions. Taking him back in memory to his Indefatigable days made his eyes dance and shine. It had been a wonderful conversation and I shall ever remember him. A few months after recording these memories I was privileged to see Billy 'over the side' for his final voyage and was able to retell his story. Indefatigable had truly rescued Billy Maclean and the boy became a man.

Young Harry Traynor on board Custodian off Greece
and on the way to Crete

Captain Harry Traynor is now the Chairman of the Indefatigable Old Boys Association and a personal friend. At the tender age of thirteen years and two months he joined Indefatigable in May, 1939. He recalls that his parents paid 13 shillings and six pence a month (half a week's wage) during his time on board. Life was hard for the young boys, no shoes were worn summer or winter, but boots were allowed for the Sunday parade and going ashore. At the outbreak of war, the lads took turns to be on watch for aircraft, standing on sandbags and ordered to blow a whistle when the enemy was in sight. There was little heat on board. That winter of 1939 - 40 was very cold, the Mersey was frozen with ice-flows. The great game was to ride on them like rafts! After lights out, the old watchman, Ted Highway (a survivor from the Titanic), kept a firm hand on the boys. If there was any noise he would turn everyone out to climb up one side of the mast and down the other. They became quite adept at this because the last one down received six cuts of the cane. The wartime cooking was done by the lads with a chef keeping a sharp watch.

Captain Traynor recalled the fun of the boat races and happy discipline of pulling together as a crew. One morning at 2 am a Swordfish Naval Aircraft was seen to crash in the river and a boat crew towed the machine to the ship, rescuing the pilot and the observer. It was a bad night and a job well done.

After only one year and one month in Indefatigable and aged fourteen and three months, Harry Traynor in what can only be described as a 'Pier Head jump' joined the Harrison Line's Custodian with the princely salary of four pounds a month. In no time the ship was at Alexandria and travelled the north coast of Africa dropping off jerry-cans of water for General Wavell's troops in the desert. The next task was to sail to Greece to pick up the 64th Royal Medium Regiment, Royal Artillery remnants which had suffered badly ... they were mostly from Liverpool ... and then they dropped them off on Crete just in time to meet the German paratroops who were to capture the island. It was here that Harry 'enjoyed' his fifteenth birthday! There were many near misses from German and Italian aircraft and twenty-eight Merchant Ships were lost.
Coincidence is certainly stranger than fiction. When the Custodian arrived safely back in Alexandria, almost the first person that Harry met when he came ashore was his father, a cook aboard the troopship

Alcantara. They had last met at home early in 1940 and Harry's dad did not know that his young son was a sea.
"What are you doing here, son?"
"Looking for Germans, dad!"
They were to meet next at the end of 1941. His father was in the Military Hospital, which we now know as the Southport Floral Pavilion.

Of the boys on Indefatigable during Harry's year thirty-three were to lose their lives and three became prisoners-of-war ... one in Germany and two in Japan.

Captain Harry Traynor became a master in Harrison's and fondly recalls that there were at least a half dozen other 'Inde' boys in command in that Company. They were proud to be 'Inde' lads

The last voyage

The new Indefatigable was in full use as a training ship until 1941, when it was decided to evacuate her because the Germans were bombing Merseyside. The old ship was sold to Messrs. T. and W. Ward for breaking up and was towed in June 1941 to Preston Slipway, but as her hull was still in remarkable good condition she was acquired by the Admiralty (not to fight!) for use as a store ship in the Clyde and renamed Carrick II. After the war she was towed again on the 20th January, 1947, to Preston to be broken up after 64 years at sea.

1941 saw the final departure of the training ships off the Sloyne at Rock Ferry. It was truly the beginning of a new chapter, but certainly not the end of the training of young seafarers. The Merseyside story was to continue in new surroundings, yet the Merseyside interest was not to diminish.

Chapter Seven

North Wales

Temporary premises were quickly found at Clwyd Newydd, near Ruthin. A very old friend of mine, Ron Wilkinson, spent some time in the new camp and I have recorded his memories. Ron's father had been lost in November 1941 when his ship, Nova Scotia, had been torpedoed off East Africa ... only 14 of the crew were saved out of a total of 114.

"We were interviewed in the old Sailors' Home where 'Bandy' Williams gave about a dozen of us a written exam. They sent us by train to Chester and then on to Ruthin. There was no-one to meet us so we all started walking, but the Captain's wife then appeared with a car and picked a few up at a time. Next day we were kitted-out in our sailors' rig. Life was tough in those huts, rough and ready and very cold. I believe the place had been the Merseyside Children's Holiday Camp. I arrived there in March 1944 and it was no holiday.

"We were divided into four divisions with about 50 in each division. We slept in two tier bunks and we were so cold. There was no heat in those huts and it was like the Arctic. I kept all my clothes on in bed and aquired as many blankets as I could. When the weather was desperate we all moved into the school room, the mess deck and the swimming area. That was a little better.

"I never forget the food. Breakfast was porridge, chunk of bread and marg and a mug of tea. Lunch was meat of some sort with potatoes and gravy, followed invariably by a sort of 'spotted dick'. Tea was pilchard pie cut into slices, two half inch chunks of bread and a mug of tea. Supper was a real rock cake and half a mug of milk. We were always starving. One day we refused to eat the stuff and in due course the chef was sacked.

"In one half of the day we did Maths and English and for the other half we worked. The mess deck had to be cleaned, the huts to be sorted, the boiler house supplied with logs ... we called the place the 'bug house'. One lad was in charge of the paint shop and the water boy looked after the pump to get the water up to the huts.

"It was early in 1945 that we moved to Plas Llanfair. Two lorries ferried some of the lads and all the property like the figurehead, the bunk beds and the ropes and that sort of stuff. The job took a week and most of us went by train.

"Llanfair was like a luxury hotel to us! Gone were the oil lamps because we actually had electric light and proper hot water. The food was much better, but I was only there two months because my time was up."

Ron was to train as an engineer and served at sea from 1950 to 1981. His elder sister, Joyce, was sadly to lose her husband, Ray, in the Piper Alpha disaster when the oil platform was destroyed by fire and explosion on the night of 6th July, 1988. Their mother, Lillie, went to sea in 1946 and spent seven years with Cunard as a stewardess. She recalled her time in the Scythia carrying displaced persons from Cuxhaven to Canada. My contact with this remarkable family was when Lillie volunteered in the early sixties to look after our Ancient Mariners' Club for retired seafarers in Kingston House. We are all much older, but still surviving and friendship and memories bind us together

Jack Harrison, 1941-42, has written his memories of his 'Inde' days.

"The bombing of Liverpool on 12th August, 1940, being the first bombs on Birkenhead, and in March 1941 magnetic mines dropped by parachute, one falling astern of Conway, the Committee following instructions from the Admiralty decided to advance the Easter Holidays and disperse the boys to their homes, those boys without parents or relatives were found accomodation in the Sailors' Home, Canning Place, Liverpool.

"Recall papers were sent out to all the boys at home May 1941 and all the boys were instructed to report to Derwen Camp, as it was called in peace time. And so the shore establishment of T.S. Indefatigable came into being.

"Summer saw the boys established in their new quarters with a healthy environment, open country, and plenty of fresh air, the Shore Establishment accepted by staff and boys alike, as well as by the local village, called Melin yr Wig, and the farming community and, of course, by the local traders.

"The day started with reveille, the night watchman being responsible for the rousing out of the galley staff and bugler. The lads went to ablutions; we never saw bacon or eggs, as far as I recollect, the porridge was mostly lumpy and tasted of the sack from which it came, but all went down with a relish. At home I wouldn't eat greens and was fussy about this and that to eat, well, after a few weeks aboard the 'Inde' I would have eaten the mess deck table. My mother couldn't get over the change in me on my first leave.

"Came the winter, 1942-43, we were installed in the swimming baths. The snow came. Snow two feet deep and frost the like of which we had never seen before. We did PT in shorts and bare feet in the stuff. Eventually, the water tower froze up and as the ablutions required water, the boys (from the shortest to the tallest) chained buckets of the liquid from the baths up to the tower on top of the hill where the officers climbed the ladders and relieved the shortage. We were frozen stiff at the finish ... proverbially brass monkey weather.

"When the good weather returned we had a nice diversion, Warship, War Bonds and National Savings weeks started up and we of the 'Inde' were picked to attend these marches through the towns and villages of Wales, Colwyn Bay, Prestatyn, Bangor, Mold, Ruthin and Buckley. We marched behind the Royal Navy followed by the other Services, always good for the boys as we were treated to a good meal after the parade. We were proud to have taken part.

"Religious service for the C of E boys were taken on Sunday mornings by Captain Superintendent W. Bambra in the mess hall. The boys of RC denomination marched to Ruthin to the Catholic Chapel, a distance from the camp of five miles. Amusement was created when passing an Italian POW Camp on the outskirts of the town, insults and banter were passed by the boys and the prisoners along with rude gestures from both sides, highlight of the day!

"Time rolled on and winter turned to spring. We had a good knowledge of Seamanship and were able to conduct ourselves as the 'Inde' had taught us. Time to leave ... some to the Royal Navy, some to the Merchant Service, others to shore establishments."

John Dickinson, 1942-43, recalls in 'The Inde' souvenir copy magazine his time in the hills of Wales under Captain W.A.Bambra, the Commander.

"I will never forget my initial introduction to the camp at Clwyd Newydd after being met at the little railway station in the valley which always seemed so far below our elevated position on the mountain summit. When I stood at the Divisional hut looking out, all compass points were downwards. Very scenic and wonderful landscape even to a child like myself who lived in and knew the countryside. Those early mornings; the crude wooden hut with double-tier bunks lining either side of the duckboarded central aisle and a single door at the far end. I now think how much it all related to the cramped quarters of the Navy's messdecks and flats."

One can assume that the last writer must have just missed that cruel winter.

.

Chapter Eight

Llanfair Pwll on Anglesey

The mansion, Plas Llanfair, which had been used by the Americans to train officers, was well adapted to become the new Indefatigable. It was a wonderful site for training and along with many friends I much enjoyed the open days when the boys were put through their paces. On occasions, I was invited to take a Padre's Hour. I talked about the Missions overseas, showed them photographs and explained the advantage of having their own club wherever they went. I also met the lads at the start of their time in Indefatigable when they arrived at the Sailors' Home in Liverpool to be 'kitted-out' under the watchful eye of Bill Hobbs. There were normally some 150 boys, aged between 13 and 16. Many of them were to enter the Services or the Merchant Navy.

Education was always the primary objective and subjects were taken up to G.C.S..E. level, together with Seamanship and General Maritime Knowledge. Uniform was worn at all times and discipline well maintained. The shore base was a vast improvement on the hardships of the old floating vessels. Times had happily changed. There were three cooked meals a day and I suspect that not one lad had ever heard of 'buzzes' and Ixion biscuits and 'burgoo' and 'spottom'!

Bernard Millichamp recalled his memories in 'the Inde' Magazine.

"I joined 'the Inde' on 5th May, 1947. I and the rest of the intake from various parts of the country had to report to the Sailors Home, Canning Street, Liverpool on the 4th May where we were given a room for the night. The following morning after breakfast we were given a written test (which I don't think anyone ever failed) set for us by one of the school teachers (Mr. Lake). Needless to say, nobody failed! After that we signed our indentures, boarded a train at Lime Street station to carry us to Llanfair Pwll on Anglesey, where we arrived quite late in the evening.

"The first sight of 'Inde' was quite awe inspiring. We approached via the back entrance nearest the station. The building loomed out of the gloom looking like Colditz Castle, with just the odd naked bulb glowing in the dark, and from one or two windows bodies would appear dressed in grey nightshirts calling out, 'Anyone from Liverpool?', or London or any other place.

"We assembled in the reception hall where I was allocated the number '109'. So I was now a 'Nozzer'. A 'Nozzer' was a new intake which lasted until the next new intake arrived; then they inherited the title.

"The worst day of the week, in my estimation, was Friday. It started as an usual type of a day - reveille at 6.45 a.m. - get washed, dressed and bunks made up - and by 7 o'clock we had to be at our allocated tasks. At 8 o'clock we lined up for breakfast as usual; but on Fridays we were treated to a large spoonful of piping hot Epsom Salts, which you had to drink down in one gulp and give your number afterwards to make sure you had swallowed it! This was followed by breakfast, then a dash to 'the heads' (toilets) to join the queue. Epsom Salts were discontinued during my stay at 'Inde'.

"After that the morning carried on like any other. Working parties and instruction. Midday was dinner (fish on Friday), followed by kit muster and bath (with the usual cold water).. Next was the doctor's muster on the messdeck. Tea was at the normal time; and at 6.30 p.m. we mustered on the messdeck for an evening with the padre (the local vicar). We usually 'plugged' for a singsong starting off with '10 Green Bottles', which we could stretch out to about '500 Green Bottles'! By the time the song was finished the poor old padre was exhausted, the reason being that he had to pump the harmonium with two foot pedals as he played. If he had been in the 'Tour de France', he'd have worn the 'yellow jersey' for the day! So ended the worst day of the week."

The Centenary Year was celebrated in 1964 and the Captain-Superintendent, Captain G.W.Irvine gave his thoughts to the Liverpool Daily Post.

"The honour bestowed upon the school by the Duke of Edinburgh in graciously consenting to visit us on this notable occasion has given us all, not only joy, but added inspiration to further our effort in training efficient seamen and good citizens

"My best wishes go to past and present boys of Indefatigable wherever they may be. I also compliment the many boys who have risen to command their own ships or who have succeeded to positions of responsibility in the Merchant and Royal Navies.

"May our long traditions of service, loyalty and self-discipline ever continue"

Many young men were to find their way into the Royal Navy for service on deck and were drafted direct to H.M.S. Ganges or H.M.S. St. Vincent, also for the Royal Marines, after passing examinations by Royal Navy examiners each month.

The school was divided into four divisions - Drake, Raleigh, Rodney and Hood - each under the charge of a divisonal officer. There were six forms, sub-divided into A and B streams, and after an initial two-week period of kitting out, marching, physical training, boating instruction and general routine, new boys were drafted into their respective forms according to academic ability, age and knowledge. They all received a sound comprehensive education up to G.C.E. level.

Captain Harry Traynor at the march-past at Llanfair

A letter received in Indefatigable on 20th June, 1982 after the Falklands campaign is a sound testimony to the discipline and training.

"Dear Captain,
I would like to thank you and Indefatigable for the training that I received in life-raft tuition.
I was aboard HMS Coventry when she was tragically hit in the Falkland Islands. I felt that the training helped a great deal in my survival and for this I am very grateful. I used to wonder what the point was for going through everything as thorough, but now the reason for it is clear.
I know that my last days in school were never wasted and I am ever thankful for them.

Yours sincerely,
Mark W. (1979 - 80)"

The spirit of adventure remained as the motivation to the last days of the school and for young boys there could be nothing more exciting than a raft race.

The Great Charity Raft Race
Certificate
1989

This certificate is to acknowledge and reward the gallant crews
Who have bravely navigated their proud vessels from the
Historic maritime centre of Portdinorwic through the waters of
The Menai Straits, defying the awesome tides and currents of
The infamous Swellies. Completing their epic voyage in the
Shelter and haven of Menai Bridge.

Indefatigable School

Signed by the President
City of
Bangor Lions

As the years passed, the merchant fleet of this country sadly diminished and this really was the end for the school. The sponsoring of boys by Local Authorities dried up and when the Gwynedd Education Authority finally withdrew its generous sponsorship of local boys, the way ahead was bleak.

Indefatigable is no longer in existence except in the memories of many old seafarers. The school closed in 1995 as the demand for sea-going had almost ceased and the original purpose lost in the changes of time. An Old Boys' Association has been formed and periodically a news letter is sent to members.

Friendships and memories of 'the Inde' will remain to the end.

H.M.S. CONWAY

'QUIT YE LIKE MEN, BE STRONG'

Chapter Nine

The School Ship Conway

The main threat to the Merchant Service in the 19th century was strangely from our own Royal Navy, because the primary method of recruiting for the Royal Navy was to impress merchant seafarers. An equal threat was the sheer incompetency of the British shipmasters.

A major step forward was in 1850 when the Board of Trade drew up an Act "for Improving the Condition of Masters, Mates and Seamen, and maintaining Discipline in the Merchant Service". In 1851 this Act became law and as a result marine boards were established in the major ports with the given task of providing a strict examination of men seeking to be masters and mates and a further task of forming boards of enquiry into marine mishaps and such problems. This Act was revised and updated in 1854.

The start of the Crimean War (1853 - 56) revealed the problem of adapting merchant seamen to the exigencies of the Royal Navy and also exposed the obvious need in the country for a merchant fleet. At the end of that conflict steps were taken to establish a long-service Navy, with pensions at the end of careers and to back the whole programme with a form of Royal Naval Reserve. This decision resulted in action in Liverpool.

In the April of 1857, Captain William Robert Mends, R.N., was appointed to command H.M.S. Hastings, which was stationed in the Mersey as the first 'District ship' to equip and train men for the Royal Navy and for the newly established, but soon to be dissolved, Royal Naval Coast Reserve. The Hastings lay in the Sloyne off Rock Ferry and cruised in the summer months for the purpose of training volunteers, visiting Caernarvon, Kirkcudbright, Anglesey and the Isle of Man. This was the catchment area for the the the 'District ship'.

All of these endeavours were not to be ignored by shipowners, who also had felt irritated by the Shipping Acts of 1851 and 1854. They were annoyed at the interference of the Board of Trade. In Liverpool, Ralph Brocklebank, a famous local shipowner, joined with Captain Judkins, of the American Royal Mail Service (later known as Cunard), to call a public meeting. Similar meetings were called in London and Southampton. In Liverpool it was resolved:
"That an Association be formed, to be called the Mercantile Marine Service Association of Liverpool and the Western Ports, and to work in close union with similar organisations in London and Southampton." This was to lead directly to the establishment of a training ship on the Mersey.

The prime mover was Captain John Clint with James Beazley as Chairman and Ralph Brocklebank, S.R. Graves, Robert Rankin and Samuel Rathbone amongst the committee members.

The committee turned to Captain William Roberts Mends, R.N., of H.M.S Hastings. There was no better person for advice and an appeal was made to the Admiralty for a ship "to train boys to become officers in the Merchant Service."

In the July, 1858, a letter was read to the Mercantile Marine Service Association (MMSA) stating that the Admiralty had offered the use of Vestal, a twenty-six gun frigate, which was lying at Chatham. However, it was discovered that fitting out Vestal would be too costly for the committee and that in fact she was probably too big for boys to handle. Happily the smaller frigate Conway, a coastguard ship at Devonport was offered instead and accepted.

This Conway, the second to bear the name on the Navy List, was a ship of six hundred and fifty-two tons when launched at Chatham in 1832. She went to sea in 1832 and served in Jamaica, the Pacific, in the Yangtze River in the Chinese War of 1840 and went to the Cape of Good Hope in 1843. She became the flagship at Portsmouth and then at Queenstown until 1857. Her last task was as coastguard ship in Devonport until she was towed by H.M.S. Virago, a six-gun paddle sloop, to the Mersey and in the evening of the 9th February, 1859 she was anchored off the Birkenhead dock wall. Then moorings were laid down near Rock Ferry slip in the Sloyne and life began as known and loved by so many seafarers.

The committee decided to equip her for 120 boys, although they limited her complement to fifty for the first six months and were prepared to spend £1,200 on her alteration and equipment. The money was raised locally from shipowners, builders, and friends of the project.

The Liverpool Mercury in May 19th,1859 published a glowing and impossibly long account of "The School Frigate Conway". Two paragraphs must suffice.
   "The boys will rise at six o'clock in the morning, wash themselves and clean the decks, and take breakfast at eight. After prayers on the main deck, one half will remain in school and the other half go on the upper deck. All will take dinner together at twelve, and after half an hour's play, teaching will be resumed from half past one to four o'clock,

the half who were above in the morning being below in the afternoon. All will take supper at five and from a quarter to six until quarter to seven o'clock they will prepare the next day's lesson in the school-room; then they will play until half-past eight, when prayers will be read, and all in bed by nine o'clock, when the ship will be inspected by the commander and chief officer. In winter these hours will be little varied. The boys will have a month's holiday at Christmas and midsummer respectively, and will be allowed to visit friends from Saturday at noon to Sunday evening on producing proper notes of invitation.

"As in the best regulated ships, the figure eight will be the basis of discipline on board. Thus there will be thirty-two (or four times eight) foretopmen, thirty-two maintopmen, and thirty-two mizentopmen; the rest being divided into forecastlemen, and afterguard; and the whole crew will be divided into messes of eight, who will dine together; and that reminds us of the dietary table, which allows per head per week seven pints of milk, seven pounds of bread, fourteen ounzes of sugar, four ounzes of butter (or cheese), one and a half pounds of flour, one pound of rice, one pound of oatmeal, five pounds of fresh meat without bone; half a pint of peas, quarter of a pound of suet, quarter of a pound of raisins, three and a half pounds of potatoes and vegetables, and tea and coffee as required; which is considered ample allowance, if not, indeed, more than be required. The uniform is blue, of fine cloth, with gilt anchor buttons, jackets with upright collars and gold braid in front of the neck, and caps bearing the badge of the Mercantile Marine Association."

The school ship was opened formally on August 1st, 1859. On the main deck was the band of H.M.S. Nile, which was visiting the Mersey on a recruitment drive. This vessel was the first 91-gun ship that ever came into the port and at the time no-one could have believed that she would eventually replace Conway and take her name. At the opening there were probably less than twenty scholars aboard. The chairman of the Mercantile Marine Association, Captain Sproule, said that he hoped that within two years they would produce a set of boys who would not disgrace any ship in the kingdom. He continued by saying how pleased he was that eminent merchants had offered to take their cadets free of charge, and to consider their training as equivalent to one year's service, thus reducing the term of apprenticeship from four years to three.

Chapter Ten

The Second Conway

By the end of the summer term of 1861 the committee found that the Conway was "much too small to afford proper accommodation for the staff and pupils, and to carry out efficiently the training and education of the boys". At the instigation of the Duke of Somerset, then First Lord, the Admiralty gave the 60-gun frigate Winchester to take the place of Conway. H.M.S.Winchester was a full-rigged ship, built at Woolwich between 1816 and 1822. With a compliment of 450, including 70 marines, she put to sea in 1822 and served as flagship in the West Indies, the East Indies, the North American station and at the Cape. She saw war service in the Indian Ocean during the Burmese War of 1852 and against pirates in the Chinese Seas in 1855. Her last task before coming to the Mersey in 1861 was in harbour service in Chatham. She was very comfortable and roomy, a beautiful ship and in the summer and early autumn was fitted out at a cost of £1,400 before taking up station off Rock Ferry. So the Winchester became the second Conway and the old Conway took the name Winchester.

At this time the American Civil War (1861 - 65) was in full swing and the Mersey was very busy. Laird had built two Armoured-Rams for the Southern States, but our Government would not allow them to be finished. These were moored very close to Conway and had to be watched during any weather. Another excitement for the cadets was the arrival of the Great Eastern, which was moored alongside. She had grounded in New York and received a rip of 150 feet, but as she had a double bottom she did not sink. Later the vessel was to lay south of Conway in the hands of the bailiffs. The cadets used to board her through her screw hole ... she had a screw and huge paddles. Sadly the vessel was broken up on the sands above New Ferry and her remains were visible until after 1890.

By 1862 there were 102 cadets on board and life had an established pattern.

"At 6 a.m. we turned out and lashed up and stowed our hammocks. We had to rush to the wash place with our basins and wait for the basins to fill from four slow-running taps: cold work in winter for the last few boys, the wash place being in the bows and the hawse pipes admitting air freely. On Tuesday and Saturday afternoons, one watch went to the Cornwallis Street swimming baths, the other to Rock Ferry. We wore gloves ashore. In those days a few minutes' walk would take us right into the country."

These written records are full of interest and one must assume that they are taken from the log books of some of the cadets, although no names are given and they form the basis of John Masefield's books on Conway.

1865-6. "I hated scrubbing the upper deck on winter mornings in bare feet. We had no sea boots. It was cold work, but doubtless was good as an hardening.

"Wednesday afternoon was a half-holiday, but the watch was only allowed within the bounds of Rock Ferry. There was a field where we tried to play cricket; it was too rough, so we had to give that up. Those who had the wherewithal spent the afternoon in the tuck shop at the head of the slip. The less fortunate spent the afternoon sitting around a coal fire at the end of the slip until it was time to return on board.

"I never knew either an officer or master to take the slightest interest in the boys out of school hours.

"The cook was known as 'Greasy Bill', and the name fitted him. He volunteered to dive off the foreyard arm in the dogwatch if we would collect sufficient sixpences. We collected enough, and Bill appeared to do his big dive. Meanwhile the chief officer got to know of this, and also appeared. Bill was sent back to his galley and all our sixpences were commandeered to buy brass-cleaning gear, so we not only lost sight of Bill having a bath, which he badly needed, but our pocket money.

1869. "One day, we were overhauling the moorings, when Conway broke adrift, and though one or two tugs tried to hold us, they could do nothing: the tide was too strong. We set the topsails, which steadied her, though the sails were very small ... she went down the river as far as the landing stage before they could bring her up. We boys were in hopes that she would go ashore, but she did not."

There was a good deal of bullying and licking with rope teasers by senior cadets. This was quite undeserved, but there was apparently little that the younger boys could do but suffer. No-one wished to complain. Another problem at this time was the inadequacy of food and this was finally solved by an enquiry in April 1873 and matters then improved.

1874. "During a very nasty winter gale an Italian barque broke adrift and collided with us on the starboard bow at night. We had to lower boats to tow her clear. It was a miserable night, blowing hard, and a hot tide running. Had we dragged our moorings, we should have been in trouble, for with the barque right on our bows we could not have let go our anchors. She got clear of us when the day dawned."

George James Brodie, Conway 1872 - 74, in the Brodie Family History included some details of his training days before he entered the Royal Navy. The Book was written around 1932.

"Before cadets joined Conway parents or guardians were provided with a prospectus containing all the rules and regulations which cadets would have to be subjected, and these were very stringent.

"There were three offences in particular which involved a very severe flogging or expulsion and these were drunkeness, desertion and theft. To be present as a spectator was almost as trying as it would have been to be flogged, and attendance of all on-board was, of course, compulsory. Prior to being flogged culprits were lashed to one of the ship's guns and the Captain (Franklin at that time. He was the ship's fourth captain, 1872 - 81 and was promoted to Rear Admiral on the retired list in 1900) addressed all present as to the nature and degree of the offence, and then gave the order to proceed with the flogging which was no ordinary birching. I was present at three such punishments ... revolting!"

Brodie pinpoints another problem at that time.
"What was desperately hard to bear was the insufficiency of food, and this lasted to about April 1873. Then it was discovered that, through illness, the junior cadets were receiving only about two thirds of the bread they should have had. In fact there was not nearly enough to go round, and what made it worse was that in each mess, first and second class petty officers and senior cadets took good care to get their 'whack' out of each loaf, and left others to fend for themselves. When an investigation was made, unlimited bread was allowed, of course, the general health and happiness was then very marked, as the food itself was plain, but good and everyone liked Conway 'duff'."

Another memory of Brodie refers to the scarlet fever attack in May 1874.
"It upset all arrangements as it was impossible to invite parents and relatives to the usual Speech day function, and when one or two deaths had occurred it was decided to send all of them home about a month earlier than usual. In July all boys free of infection returned to the ship."

It was a serious and dangerous disease. It certainly pinpointed the defects of the ship, the poor ventilation on the lower deck, the inadequacy of the isolation ward, the inferior washing facilities and general accommodation. It was obvious that the present vessel was too small and that a larger frigate or line-of-battle ship was required.

In the September of the following year Captain Webb, an old Conway, visited the ship to receive a pair of binoculars subscribed for by the cadets. Webb had swum the channel from Dover to Calais on August 24th and 25th in 21 hours 45 minutes. In honour of the visit the boys were given a half-day holiday.

Moves were well under way with the Admiralty for the gift of Nile to replace Conway. Captain Franklin, then Captain-Superintendent, was sent in July 1875 to Devonport in order to examine and report on the condition of the Nile. He proposed that the engines and boilers be removed; that she should be recaulked and painted, that iron ballast should be supplied; that all her channels, her head and hammock nettings, being defective or thoroughly delapidated, should be repaired; and that her Downtown pumps should be overhauled. This work was put in hand in the dockyard. Happily her hull was as sound as a bell.

H.M.S. Conway on the River Mersey

From the Naval and Military Gazette, June 21st, 1876.

"Valorous, paddle frigate, Captain Jones, left Plymouth Sound for Liverpool, with the Nile in tow, on the 20th inst."

June 28th, 1876. "The Nile, an old line-of battle ship intended to take the place of Conway for the Mercantile Marine Service Association at Liverpool, was towed out of Devonport Harbour, on the 20th inst. by two dockyard tugs, and was afterward taken hold of by the Valorous, six paddle frigate, Captain L.F .Jones. When the two vessels were about to leave the Sound the hawsers parted, and the Nile had to drop anchor. Two tugs were immediately despatched to render assistance."

From the Army and Navy Gazette, July 1st, 1876.

"Valorous ... arrived at Rock Ferry on the 23rd ult. with the Nile in tow from Devonport."

June, 1876. "We went into the Great Float (the West Float) at Birkenhead to change over to the Nile. That was a glorious time for us.

"I have no recollection of the boys working the capstan to unmoor the ship; probably that part was done by a mooring lighter, as it would have been heavy work to take off the mooring swivel with the old-fashioned gear. We were taken in tow by two or three tugs, to the Great Float, where the Nile was already berthed. The Conway was secured alongside her. The Nile was stripped to her three lower-masts. As all school was finished for the term, we were employed in stripping the Conway to a gantline.

"We sent down the topmasts and lower yards, and the caps from the lower-mast heads. As you can imagine, the caps were pretty well frozen on, so Tom Priestly and Wally Blair, our two maintop instructors, rigged a sort of battering-rams, called 'bumpers', which we boys worked from on deck: they were spars rigged so as to strike heavy blows on the undersides of the caps. With these we bumped the caps off.

"We lived on board the old Conway, and hoisted everything out of her with the old yard and stay tackle into the Nile, guns, masts, yards and stores of every description: it was fairly heavy work for boys, but of course we enjoyed it thoroughly and thought ourselves real sailors.

"One thing we did appreciate was the privilege of getting away from the ship after working hours and bathing from the mooring buoys. After all stores and gear had been transferred to the Nile, we went home for the summer holidays. A great deal of work had to be done on board the Nile before she was fit for a school ship."

The Nile had served on the North American and West Indian stations and had carried the flag of Sir A. Milne. In Devonport the machinery had been removed and she was ballasted with 220 tons of copper dross and 175 tons of iron. The topmast and topgallant masts, yards, rigging etc. were all in perfect order for the instruction of pupils in manning yards, and making and shortening sail. There was ample space for school rooms, a hospital, a wardroom and all other needs. The main deck was regarded as light and airy with a height of seven feet from deck to deck; it was all painted white with skylights extending over fifty feet in length and averaging ten feet in breadth. The large cooking range was forward with the cooks' and stewards' accommodation; the range had been removed from the nearby Great Eastern.

Incidentally, the old Winchester (previously Conway) six weeks after her arrival in Devonport was renamed Mount Edgecombe. She was to remain as a training ship at Devonport until at the venerable age of 104 years, she was broken up in October 1920.

On 24th July, 1876 permission was granted to the MMSA by the Admiralty to change the name Nile to Conway. After the summer holidays the new term began with the vessel moored off Rock Ferry. Some weeks were to pass before the shipwrights finished their work.

All three Conways were designed by Sir Robert Seppings who died in 1840 just a year after the launching of the Nile. The third Conway was to remain stationed off Rock Ferry for 65 years, until in 1941 she was moved to Bangor in the Menai Straits, North Wales.

Chapter Eleven

The Third Conway

Life continued with the normal set routines and, with more space available, the numbers grew to 163. One innovation was the introduction of paraffin lamps. They were high risk and much time was spent in experimenting with new fire extinguishers. It was very dangerous and the resulting inevitable fires were put out with buckets of sand.

One cadet wrote as follows: "We had a new steward on board. I do not know his name, all we knew him by was Hungry. When at church service we sang 'He hath filled the hungry with good things,' we would shout out Hungry. At last the captain stopped the service at this point and gave us a good talking to."

The cadets continue their stories.

1880. "The Sugar Shop. One boy conceived a brilliant idea! Brown sugar from our old friend 'Mother Taylor' cost two and a half pence per pound. This boy transferred some of his clothes to his pal's chest, and forthwith started a grocer's shop. The pound of sugar was split up into five 'whacks' at a penny - 100 per cent profit. This did not last long. Rival tradesmen stepped in, dividing the pound into four 'whacks', followed by others who made it only three. Other eatables were introduced. For some time, cake merchants did a good trade. Jam, cocoa and milk, Nestle's condensed milk and so on followed. Alas, Captain Franklin discovered what was going on, and all the grocers' shops were stopped.

"At the end of every term we were warned that no-one was to throw his mug down the hold. But the old custom prevailed. What a glorious noise 150 mugs made when flung to smash from the main deck to the lower hold.

"I remember going back after a Christmas holiday, in February 1881 or 1882, and arriving at Rock Ferry in late afternoon, with a gale blowing, a sea running and large blocks of ice in the river. I got into the steam launch, but one boat, full of boys and their chests, was unable to fetch the ship, and late at night landed on the mud beyond New Ferry, the hands had to wade ashore in ice and mud, spend all night as best they could and come off next day."

Much has been written and could be written about the school ship Conway. A correspondent some twenty five years after the arrival of Conway in the Mersey gives a lively picture. The year is 1883. The writer is not identified.

"One bright morning last Autumn I found myself on the Rock Ferry slip. Four line-of-battle-ships, 'hearts of oak', strangely thick and heavy looking in comparison with an iron-clad Cunard liner lying near them, were anchored out in the broad river, and I was waiting for a boat from one of them.

"Presently a cutter, manned by thirteen smart boys ... the inevitable bull must be excused, for the boys are learning to do men's work ... came to shore, but not for me. A Police Officer landed from it, and, seeing him drop something heavy, bright, and gruesome into his pocket, I understood that he must have come from the Clarence or the Akbar. On inquiry it appeared that he had been to both ships, leaving four juvenile offenders on the one floating reformatory and two on the other, to be trained for honest seamen in the three coming years. Let us wish them and their two or three hundred companions all success. Looking at the crew of this boat (it was from the Akbar, the Protestant reformatory ship, but one from the Clarence would have presented much the same appearance) one could see that the law was giving these boys a noble chance of reaching honourable manhood.

"A few minutes later, another cutter came in, crowded with about thirty boys of quite different style, the sons of happier mothers. Half of them leaped ashore, in good order but eagerly; well-dressed, gentlemanly looking lads, and hastened off to enjoy their Saturday holiday. Some who carried tidy little valises were not to return until Monday morning .... but the crew of their companions who brought them in were not to take me out, for that was the mail boat, and must perform its proper function punctually.

"The leave-boys were scarcely out of sight when a handsome barge of sixteen oars drew up at the pier in splendid style. "Fenders out! Port oars in!" shouted the coxswain, and the boat lay ready for me, with eight oars perpendicular and the stern sheets gay with crimson cushions. The bit of water was crossed swiftly, and we were brought to the side of the Conway with that dextrous precision which tells of discipline, active hands and clear eyes.

"Arrived on the upper deck, you find the Akbar to be your nearest neighbour, the Clarence the remotest of the four. Between these lies the Indefatigable, of which a word must be said. It is not a reformatory, but receives the orphans of seamen, sons of struggling widows, adventurous boys who will go to sea, and whose friends seek by two or three years' training here to give them a much better chance of success.
"The distinctive position of the Conway will by this time be

understood. It is a school for the sons of gentlemen, taking that much-abused word as representing a certain social status, and is intended to give them such education as shall make them gentlemen in education and personal character. To this extent it is the same as many another boarding-school.

"I shall refrain from any attempt to describe the good ship, standing in wholesome dread of the ridicule which might be incurred by very probable mistakes in the use of nautical terms.

"The Commander, every inch a gentleman and a sailor, has had experience in both the Merchant and the Royal Navy, and conducts the business of the ship with enthusiasm. His post can be no sinecure, involving as it does the care by day and night of some 170 spirited lads; but his efforts, heartily seconded by an excellent staff of teachers and officers, seemed decidedly successful. The discipline is strict, but that is no fault; and it is enforced and accepted with good will.

"I ventured to ask the Commander, as we were standing on the poop, to give orders for 'Fire quarters', an amusement to me of rather a fascinating character. Calling a lad, he directed him to ring the fire-bell, and whispered that the scene of fire was to be the lower deck aft. Instantly on the second stroke following the alarm the lads ran helter-skelter from the places where they had been reading, playing, writing home letters, working, to their appointed stations, a particularly bright young gentleman taking his place at the Commander's elbow as his messenger. Going to the main deck and the lower deck with the dignity of a 'special' (not to say of a Commander) we found ports and scuttles closed, crews standing by each boat with the tackle for lowering it in their hands, fire-engines, pumps and hose rigged and manned; and as we neared the spot where the fierce enemy was supposed to have begun his attack, rows of lads, each with a full bucket at his feet, and a smothering party, each of whom had a hammock on his shoulders ready for prompt application. Everything was done, without a word spoken and quite within four minutes, precisely as if a fire had been a real one, except that I was relieved to find that the port-watch of the forecastlemen (the smothering party) had not proceeded to the serious extremity of wetting their hammocks for my entertainment. An operation like this, performed swiftly and thoroughly and withal very suddenly, by 150 boys, is satisfactory proof of the training and discipline which renders it possible.

"The life on board seems to be pleasant. Six hours of direct study, with drill in the practical operations of seamanship connected with masts, sails, and ropes, leave plenty of time for amusements between rising at six and going to bed at nine. I was so unfortunate as to miss a Christy Minstrels' entertainment which has taken place on the evening preceeding my visit, and the laughter from which had not quite died away the next forenoon. The solemn presentation of razors, among other things, to the two chief prizemen of the School, about to leave, seems to have furnished no little mirth. Lectures, concerts, and the like are frequent after the days have grown too short for cricket and football on shore."

The cadets continue the tale.

1882 - 4.   "A boat's crew returning from the slip missed the ship in the dark owing to the very strong tide and wind. It got later and later, and there was no sign of the boat, and we all gathered around the gangway anxiously waiting for news of her. We could see that the officers were anxious. Suddenly the chaplain appeared, and the ship was piped for prayers; after these we sang the sea hymn, 'Eternal Father Strong to Save,' which by the way was sung every Sunday. By and by, we heard that the boat had been sighted, pulling up inshore where the current was weaker, so as to get well ahead before striking out for us in another attempt to fetch the ship. As she was slanted off to us, the barrel-buoy and life-line were hove overboard and veered out to her; the boat caught it, the line was snatched through a block on the lower deck, we manned it and walked her up to the ship. The instructor and boat's crew were wet through and exhausted but had stuck to their work and refused to stay on shore for the night because they knew that all on board would have been anxious had they failed to return.

"I have always remembered that night, the lower deck lighted by the oil lamps then in use, the wet line coming in, and the boys all putting their weight on to it as they walked it in, and the cheer for the dripping boat's crew when they trod the deck with safety. The Captain's 'Well done, boys' and the order to 'Carry on', 'Sling hammocks', ended what might have been a tragic night.

The morning wash

"In those days, a large full-rigged ship H.M.S. Defence, the guardship, lay just off the slip, to seaward from us. We were then second in the line, Defence, Conway, Akbar, Indefatigable and Clarence.

"Two important events have taken place on board the good old ship within a month. The first was the highly interesting and instructive Lecture on the 'Great Ice Age,' by Sir Robert Ball, the eminent Astronomer-Royal for Ireland. By the aid of the powerful oxy-hydro light, the lecturer was able to convey to the minds of the cadets the wonders of the pre-historic age, when the great ice king reigned supreme over much of the surface of the earth. So much was told to the boys on the subject as to engage their thoughts for the rest of the term, if strict attention was paid to what fell from the lecturer's lips. The other event was perhaps the most acceptable to the boys, being always welcomed with outbursts of joy ... the 'Break-up Supper'. This time-honoured custom on the Conway is an occasion of much festivity, and is almost as eagerly looked forward to by the invited guests as by the boys. The attendance is always good, when weather permits, and the programme generally includes an Entertainment by the boys, dancing on the main deck led by the Indefatigable band, with the Supper at the conclusion. The evening of the 19th saw a goodly company assembled on the old frigate, both guests and boys 'footing it right merrily' to the inspiring strains of the band. Then followed the Supper, marked as usual by those spirited speeches which are looked upon as one of the most notable events of the evening. The ever popular Commander leads off with his address to the boys, his speech being delivered in his own free and hearty style. Mr. Clarke Aspinall (who honoured the company with his presence at some little inconvenience to himself, having come specially from Manchester for the occasion) gave one of those rattling speeches which always seem to 'hit' the mark wherever he goes. Altogether the 1887 Supper was a great success - excelling, perhaps, even those of years gone by - and it was with regret that the guests were reminded by the lateness of the hour that it was time to return ashore."

The Gale, November 1st, 1887.

"It came on to blow and a big sea got up: the Conway rolled like a wash-tub, and many of us were seasick. Several of the Runcorn schooners parted their cables on the ebb and drifted past us: one of them smashed new Ferry pier; another passed close to us, out of control, with no-one on deck: she smashed our swinging boom and passed on. Two of these schooners sank at Birkenhead and lost some of their hands.

"At about the middle of the forenoon, the Akbar began to drag; she drifted close alongside of the Conway, did not harm us, but carried away her own quarter davits and boats. The two old wooden walls lay or rather rolled alongside each other, almost scraping the paint off each other's sides. Both ships hoisted signals of distress.

"At this point, one of the gunpowder flats, which had broken from her moorings at Eastham, came drifting down straight for the small gap between the Conway and the Akbar. A hulk full of gunpowder grinding in between two old line-of-battle ships might have led to unpleasant fireworks. Luckily, the Firefly, the ferry-boat, managed to get a line aboard the powder-flat, and towed her on to the mud at New Ferry. When the weather moderated a little, two tugs got the Akbar away from us and into the Birkenhead Docks."

Recreation included trips to local holiday resorts including Llandudno in North Wales. On 20th April 1889 aboard the steaming Sea King, the band from the training ship Indefatigable was enlisted. The conditions were not what they could have been.

"The steamer, the tug Sea King, left the the Conway at about nine o'clock, and proceeded to the Indefatigable to take up the band belonging to that ship. She then went down the river and out by the Crosby Channel. The sea was rather rough at the bar and it caused the boat to pitch about a good deal. Some of the Conway fellows, and many of the Indefatigables were seasick. The 'band' being no longer worthy of the name, having indeed become for the time quite 'disbanded', and lying about in every direction." (The Cadet Vol 1.)

1890 - 92. "These were bad years for the ship; she got into a stagnant way: and as no impulse towards improvement came from above, many other impulses came from below. There was much discontent on board, with some attempts at mutiny, and several successful conspiracies for the destruction of ship's property."

John Masefield was actually a Conway cadet from 1891 to 1894 and his writing reflects life on board at this time. His book The Conway was written in 1933 and was revised and updated in 1953. In 1944, Masefield published an account of his Conway years and it is entitled New Chum. Life had not been easy. His gift for describing the river at that time tells the story.

"We watched ships being built and launched and floated. We saw them going forth in splendour and coming back shattered by the sea, listed, shored up, dismasted, red with sea-rust, white with sea salt, holed, dinted, ruined, all pumps still spouting, just limping into dock with three tugs, or just crawling to the mud and lying down."

And still these young lads chose the sea!

Life continued aboard H.M.S.Conway for the many thousands of cadets who were trained for command. It was the well tried mixture of seamanship, discipline and hard work. At dawn the diesel generators would rumble into action, followed half an hour later by the bugle for reveille. Then came the command for all hands to bathrooms and a speedy lashing and storage of hammocks. "All hands clean ship!" Off went the first boats to collect the catering staff from shore and the tables were rigged for breakfast. All too soon was heard the pipe, "Rig school!" and another day in Conway had started.

1895. "The Mersey was a sheet of ice from bank to bank. About 9.30 in the evening of December 17th, the night before the beginning of the Christmas holidays, the Conway's north mooring chain (of iron links three inches square) parted on a flood tide, and the ship dragged her other anchor till she was alongside the Akbar. Rockets were at once sent up. All hands were called and sent to stations for letting go anchors; some tugs came promptly alongside and after some bargaining the Skirmisher and Firefly got hawsers aboard and the ship was held."

The vessel was then taken to Bidston Graving Dock and stripped of her copper, scraped, recaulked, refelted and recoppered. Ten to fifteen tons of mussels and sea-grass were taken off her copper, which was paper-thin in many places. The work was done by hundreds of shipwrights.

In the early hours of July 26th, 1899, the Clarence was destroyed by fire and happily all of the two hundred and thirty-five boys escaped safely. The lesson was well learned aboard Conway and the fire precautions were overhauled and a fire tank holding 4,500 gallons was built in, seven feet above the upper deck, and fitted with pipes to each deck.

Chapter Twelve

The New Century

On the 7th May, 1903, Captain Archibald Miller died of diabetes in his cabin and the chief officer, Captain Harvey Broadbent, succeeded to command. In the July His Majesty King Edward the Seventh visited Liverpool to lay the foundation stone of the Anglican Cathedral. Of more importance to the cadets, the galley was remodelled with new ranges, the shore sanatorium was improved, six acres of ground were bought for playing fields, a good Rugby ground was created and for the first time in the history of the school, hockey was played. A new spirit swept though the ship. A short while after a tennis court and pavilion appeared.

1906 "I kept clear of Bertie Chip, who was the second officer, and about the only time when we really came into conflict was when he had to muster my chest. As I was not very smart at getting my gear out he turned the whole chest upside down, and I got a good cuff if I did not produce the article smartly when he read it out from the list.

"In those days each boy supplied his own knife, fork and spoon. The juniors sat at the bottom of the mess, with the result that they got what was left and if it needed cutting it had to be done with a clasp knife and eaten with the fingers, as the cutlery disappeared the first time it was brought up. All this however was speedily changed by Monty Douglas when he succeeded Bertie Chip."

1911.   "In spite of the lovely summer weather, the ship's company suffered in June from a severe attack of influenza, in which at one time over forty boys were laid up out of the two hundred on board. The general holiday granted to all hands on account of the King's Coronation was prolonged to twelve days. This ended the epidemic."

After the declaration of war in 1914, the ship entered upon difficult years, of training many young officers for the Royal Naval Reserve with greatly depleted staffs.

"Captain Broadbent at first sight was a terrifying man whose look froze you to the deck. When inspecting divisions with his tongue pressing out his cheek his set glare made one shudder, but one got to accept his little mannerisms and although held in great respect he endeared himself to all. I remember in the finals of the light weights, Mrs. Broadbent remarked that '....'s eye is closed up'. 'Well, what about it?' said Captain Broadbent, 'he can see out of the other one.' "

1916. March 4th.   "We parted from our moorings (the starboard bridle chain to the swivel broke), and nearly went ashore below Rock Ferry slip. It was at noon, on a big spring tide, with the ship swinging. We had an epidemic of mumps on board at the time and were very short of hands. However, we did not go ashore, the port anchor was let go, and we were brought up in deep water and held in position all night by the salvage craft, who docked us that night in the West Float. There was a crowd at pierhead to see us go up the Float in the morning. One among the crowd cried: 'What in hell is this? Is this the Victory?' The commander (Dibb) who was on the fo'c's'le, in charge, forward, shouted: 'Yes, she is. And I'm Lord Nelson!' "

During the war there were on average well over 200 cadets on board and life was hard.

"In February, 1917, I remember ice floes in the river, sometimes the pinnace became so jammed between blocks of drifting ice that her hands could get out and walk about.

"On Sunday mornings, in the winter and spring of 1918, it was the pride of the starboard mizentop to 'rig church' in a minute and a quarter. We were on the hatches, mustered and ready, but off the deck. When the pipe went, each man knew exactly his job, the co-ordination was perfect, and in a minute and a quarter the transformation was complete: altar-rails shipped, benches and chairs in place, altar decked and the harmonium ready.

"After breakfast, we were allowed two and a quarter minutes to lash and stow our hammocks."

Armistice day, Monday, November 11th, 1918.
"Up as usual. Breakfast. School. At 11.10 a.m. came the news that the Armistice was signed. Immediately we started cheering. Of course the masters could not do anything. At last the head came up and the bell was struck for silence. Then we gave three hearty cheers and sang 'God Save the King', and then cheered more. Then we went on pretending to work. Everyone was very excited.

"Meanwhile every ship in the river let off her siren and made a most unearthly row. From Liverpool and Birkenhead docks came a tremendous growl and roar as all the sirens blended their sounds into one."

In 1921 there was a Spring coal strike and the boiler had to cease work: The ship went without electric light and hot water. The Downton pumps, though over eighty years old, came back into use for the salt-water tanks; and the old cries of 'Heave round, fore and after Downtons' were heard again.

1927.   On March 31st a presentation was made to Captain Broadbent on his retirement after twenty-nine years' service on board (twenty-five in command). He was succeeded by Captain F.A. Richardson, D.S.C., R.N., an Old Conway.

"Captain Richardson, as a captain, was always very much above the ordinary. He had a kind heart and knew a fair amount about boys. In my fifth term I was 'canteen merchant' and when I turned the keys over to him last thing at night he or Mrs. Richardson nearly always had a spare supper for me. How welcome it was!

"I also remember Captain Richardson for the thoroughness with which he made rounds on Sunday mornings. His white gloves were in every nook and cranny and woe betide the captain of the top if they came away dirty.

"Between 'heave round' on Saturday and the captain's inspection of the ship after morning 'divisions' on Sunday certain parts of the ship were jealously protected as 'holy ground'. On the main deck for example that part of the deck where the captain stood at 'divisions' and where the altar was placed for the Sunday service was scrubbed white and protected for the next twenty-four hours by benches placed round it.

"The recipe for the liquid used to clean 'holy ground' was one handful of soft soap, one of 'soojie' (soap powder), half a bucket of hot water added and steam from the boiler passed through the mixture. It was applied with a hand-scrubber and on bended knee. Glass was cleaned with dry crumpled newspaper and one's breath, and I never found better substitutes."

1931.   "The most thrilling incident of my time happened during the Easter term. It had been a quiet day; the Last Post had been sounded and everybody turned in. Suddenly we heard the clang of the fog-bell, and knew that it had come on thick.

"About midnight the two cadet captains on fog-watch noticed a red light bearing down upon us. A boy in the starboard fore, who happened to be awake, saw the light through the forward port, leapt out of his hammock and dashed up the fore hatch. Instantly there was a loud grating crash and the fog-watch reported to the officer of the watch that a coasting vessel had rammed us. A boy sleeping on the lower deck yelled out in terror as the anchor cable jumped in the air and smashed some of the washing basins to pieces. Every one on the orlop deck turned out forthwith. The fo'c's'lemen at once hove on the compressor-falls because they thought that the anchor cable might have broken under the impact.

"On the lower deck all the deck lights were on, screens up and gangway doors open. On the starboard gangway an officer signalled to the coaster, but apparently nobody on the coaster could understand the message. However, after a lot of yelling the coaster proceeded up to the Manchester Ship Canal.

"We lost our dolphin striker and our bows were badly damaged; the coaster had her mainmast broken and plates badly bent."

1934.   Captain F.A. Richardson left the ship at the beginning of June after seven years of service in Conway. The command was taken by Captain T.M. Goddard, Lieutenant-Commander of the South African Naval Service, old Conway 1905 - 07. He had commanded the South African Training Ship General Botha in 1921.

1935.   "Hoppy Lee when I joined the ship was the senior warrant officer, he used to wear the Conway uniform with two stripes and a diamond. He kept watches with the first and second lieutenants, and taught us seamanship. I am certain that he was an old Conway because he loved the ship more than anyone else that I ever came across. He had a short leg which I believe he got in some kind of accident in sail. When he retired as a watch-keeper he became seamanship master to the ship, and he must have retired sometime during the war. I met him one day in the last years of the war in the Wirral where he was engaged in making some kind of a stove to burn sludge oil. He recognised me on sight, and remembered, much to my surprise, my name. We had a fine old yarn."

H.M.S. Conway Docking at Birkenhead

1937. "During this term an overhaul was being planned. Examination had showed that the heat of the cooking-range in the course of some sixty years had done damage to the main-deck beams and deck-sheathing near the galley. Beams and decking had to be renewed, and the coal-burning range changed for a coke-burning slow-combustion cooker. Two beams near the main hatch (main deck) had sagged. The planking of the hull needed some renewal here and there, about 550 square feet in all. It was judged that all the outer plank should be cleared of paint; the ship shut down, save for watchmen, and the upper copper examined.

"The ship was towed to Vittoria Dock, Birkenhead in the forenoon of July 29th. When the paint was removed from the planking, the need for re-caulking was found to be pressing. All the main planking above L.W.L. to two planks above the lower deck was caulked and pitched. The worst of the main planking was removed and renewed. When the planking was removed, it was found that on the whole the timbering was in excellent condition.

"The oak used in the replacements was English oak, felled for five years and really sound, as indeed English oak is ... it has a beauty and distinctivness all its own, most apparent when compared with foreign oak .. its durability is amazing. The oak used in the ship in this overhaul was said to have come from Shropshire, and to have been at least 400 years old. The ship returned to her moorings on September 13th, in time for the new term."

In dry dock

At the end of the term the ship was returned to Birkenhead to be dry-docked. This was a serious task as there was fear that she would simply break in two when she came down upon the blocks. However, all was well.

The last time that the copper sheathing had been replaced was in 1896 and by this time (December 1937) much of it had perished, although the felting had remained firm. When examined the hull was found to be in excellent condition, but there was still work to be done. All the planking was cleaned and trimmed, and all butts caulked and pitched. This entailed 16,000 feet of caulking, or well over three miles of seam, into each inch of which oakham had to be driven. All the under-water hull was coated with a mixture of Stockholm tar and pitch, then covered with felt and resheathed with sheets of new copper. The total cost was £20,000, of which £5,000 was generously given by Alfred Holt and Company.

A few months later she was back in dock for more repairs and above all to receive a new figurehead, to replace the old one which had been carried away twenty years before by the S.S.Bhamo. The jib-boom was replaced immediately after the accident. The ship's original figurehead was certainly Lord Nelson, yet it was generally understood to be Lord Collingwood. Captain Broadbent, who had salvaged pieces after the accident admitted to uncertainty.

The new figurehead was carved from a four-ton block of teak by Mr. E. Carter Preston. It represented Nelson in admiral's uniform and stood thirteen and a half feet high. After the unveiling on Sunday, September 11th, the cadets attended a special Merchant Navy service in Liverpool Cathedral.

On 28th June, 1939, (the anniversary of the original launching in 1839) there were many visitors on board. A brass band provided the entertainment as tea and refreshments were served. After that all hands fell-in by divisions on the upper deck, facing aft. Captain Goddard gave a brief speech to mark the moment of the launch one hundred years before.

3rd September, 1939 was the start of the Second World War and life on board changed. The lads off Indefatigable blacked-out all white paint work, fitted concrete covers to the hatches and all skylights and covered the upper deck with sand-bags. 130 windows had to be darkened. Conway was ready to face the war.

Chapter Thirteen.

The Final Years on the Mersey

Outbreak of war in September 1939 brought with it a call for more men. The Conway made prompt answer. In peacetime a compliment of 180 cadets was considered maximum, but throughout hostilities this figure was increased to 250 to suit likely candidates for the Royal Air Force and the Fleet Air Arm as well as the Royal and Merchant Navies.

Old Boys of the ship reached high executive posts in every theatre of war and gained honour and renown on the sea and under the sea, on land and in the air. In the First World War 1,450 Old Boys are known to have served in the Forces, quite apart from the many hundreds who served in the Merchant Sevice. 170 Old Boys are known to have been killed, and the decorations won include three V.Cs, 36 D.S.Os, 102 D.S.Cs, M.Cs, and D.F.Cs. In the Second World War the record was well maintained … four reached the rank of Admiral, and two that of Air Vice-Marshal, 166 were killed and the honours included one V.C, one George Cross,

22 D.S.Os, 40 O.B.Es, 99 D.S.Cs, 2 M.Cs, 20 D.F.Cs, one G.M., 12 M.B.Es., 4 A.F.Cs and one B.E.M. This is truly a remarkable record.

The everyday story of life aboard in wartime continued.

"Next term we watched ships loading and unloading at close quarters, and sometimes getting a pocket-full of monkey-nuts from kindly stewardesses. The thrill of helping a naval auxiliary to berth and being invited aboard, a topic of conversation for weeks. And then the excitement of the trip back to Rock Ferry. Air-raids, 'abandon ship', in the middle of the night and going ashore in the cutter with an impressive stick of bombs falling off Cammell Laird's. Next day on board to collect gear and the sight of a straggling stream of cadets carrying hammocks up to Rock Ferry station, dropping soup plates, hair-brushes, etc., out of them en route!"

Another cadet wrote of those days.

"During the heavy bombing of Liverpool, there were weeks when the only rest I got was in an uncomfortable camp bed at the after end of the main deck during the lulls in the bombing. I would never turn in during an air-raid warning, but never missed divisions even after the wildest night.

"As to the food: well, it was war-time; but it left lots to be desired. We had many names for it; sodduk for bread, grease for butter, D.M.T. (Dead Man's Toe) for a steamed roly poly pudding and so on."

Commander G.B.W. Johnson, RNZN, Conway 1940 - 42, has recorded extracts from his diary of those eventful years.

"I remember seeing the masts of H.M.S. Hood down river, and on another occasion I went, with other cadets, on board the first American four-funnel destroyer to arrive in the Mersey ... one of the first of fifty acquired by Britain." His diary then continues rather casually.
"July 20. Heave round in the morning; went ashore in afternoon for a

walk with Jones and bought a little tuck; coaster crashed into the boom and 10-oared cutter; not much damage done.

"July 21. Church in morning; went out in No.1 motor boat to watch a gig race; church and baths later; air-raid in the evening.

"1941. March 13 Saw two bombs fall in the Mersey. Nazi plane shot down. Mine dropped near ship; went ashore to Royal Rock Hotel about 2 a.m., came back about 8 a.m.; air-raid damage ashore, bad; mine sinks a City boat; we came to Parkgate."

The last few paragraphs give a sample of the almost casual observations of the port at war and as we see a little later actually led to the departure of Conway to the safety of Menai Straits. That story will be told by Captain Goddard.

We continue the story through the eyes of the cadets.

"1940. November 12th. At midnight in a stormy dark night, during an air-raid and a strong ebb tide, the 13,000 ton whale-factory ship S.S Hektoria with a full cargo of whale-oil on board dragged her anchors, sheered down upon the ship's bow, near the port fore-chains, and stuck there, being unable to get clear. Aboard Conway all hands turned out, and made all clear for letting go both anchors. The thrust of the collision had started the Conway's S.E. mooring-anchor. The two ships dragged down to the Rock ferry pontoon together before the visitor could draw clear. Next day the ship was towed into Vittoria Dock for repairs."

Captain Jim Thompson, Conway 1939 - 41, recalls the Hektoria incident.

"I was in my hammock slung on the Lower Deck at the time and heard Captain Goddard, who was standing at the head of the Starboard gangway call out, 'Wah, fwend her off with bwoomsticks'!

Cdr and Mrs Goddard

"There was always danger on the river as yet another collision occurred and was recorded in the log. I remember the collision. It was blowing a full gale at the time, and even the shelter of the Mersey could not offer much protection. A large 20,000 ton tanker was moored at what should have been a perfectly safe distance from us. By nightfall the gale's full force was felt. As the tide changed we swung to our moorings and the tanker, which had undoubtedly been dragging anchor was uncomfortably near to us. By this time all hands were turned in, but not for long - as the gale raged the tanker continued to drag.

"All hands were piped shortly after a rending crash, as the monster slid past our starboard side catching only our starboard boom."

Conway was to remain in dock until Sunday, March 9th, 1941 and during that time (November - March) there were fifteen air-raids, lasting altogether sixty-nine hours. The strain on the ship's company was immense as they endured extra watches and fire-watches. These raids were nothing to the raids that were to follow on Merseyside. Fortunately the Conway with her strong timbers could stand near misses from bombs which exploded in the water. On two occasions sticks of bombs straddled the vessel and that would have been near enough to start the rivets in a steel ship. The log continued the saga.

"I was aboard during the bombing. We spent our nights on watches, dealing with incendiary bombs which had a nasty habit of landing on our decks night after night. I was surprised the way they penetrated the inch boarding over the chartroom on the upper deck; we used to scoop them over the side on shovels until told that this was a dangerous method, so we then treated them with respect as taught to the air-raid wardens. The night I remember most was the night that the mines came down, one mooring itself just ahead of us and several around the stern. As the tide was ebbing, it was thought that on the turn the ship might connect with one. In the middle of the night we abandoned ship."

1941. March. An enemy aircraft flew over the ship from Rock Ferry, heading for South Liverpool. Two parachute magnetic mines were dropped and one fell alongside the nearby S.S. Tacoma City whilst the other drifted slowly over Conway and fell twelve yards short of her. Captain Goddard immediately ordered, yet again 'Abandon ship'. The Captain wrote "The cadets were excellent and for once were really quiet. They dressed quickly and went to the stations. Within twenty minutes from the time of calling, just over 200 cadets and staff including my wife and our Siamese cat, which made more noise than anyone or everyone, were on the Rock Ferry pontoon. They made their way to Conway House, the Royal Rock Hotel, and the Royal Mersey Yacht Club House where they were kindly entertained and housed." Captain Goddard continued the story.

"At about 1.30 p.m., the Tacoma City was changing over her dynamos. The mine which fell ahead of her had drifted down with the tide and had grounded under her bottom ... the magnetic mine exploded, sinking the ship in a few minutes." Conway's No. 1 motor-boat, with Lieutenant Brooke-Smith in charge, picked up the forty-five members of her crew including the captain.

"By this time arrangements had been made to accommodate the cadets in Mostyn House School at Parkgate. When all were on board they were told to lash-up in their hammocks a plate, cutlery and sports gear, and proceed to the station with all speed. It was a never-to-be-forgotten sight, to see small mizzen-topmen staggering under the weight of huge hammocks up Bedford Road and the commander urging them into the train while the guard was blowing his whistle.

"That evening, two hundred odd cadets were most kindly received at Mostyn House School. They were organised into messes and dormitories and promptly turned-in; the schoolboys sleeping in the air-raid shelter. After a few days it was decided to close the term, send the boys home, and try to find alternative moorings for the ship in a safer place."

The solution was found. Off Bangor was the empty berth of the old H.M. screw corvette Clio. It took two months to renew the moorings and under wartime pressures find two tugs for the voyage. Life was hard. The enemy made a desperate attempt to close the port of Liverpool. That first week in May were the worst as Merseyside (just a north-west port in the news) suffered continuous and severe bombing. Our country has never really understood the fortitude and sheer endurance of the people of Merseyside during those times. The damage and loss of life was horrendous, yet Conway survived, as did Liverpool. At 3 p.m., May 21st, 1941, the ship was prepared to leave the Sloyne in tow of the Langarth and Dongarth. The naval patrols had been warned that a hulk was to proceed under tow. It was a dull and wet evening as at 6.21 p.m. she slipped her last bridle and moved off at slack water with the tugs ahead. The Rock Ferry Pontoon rang its bell and many ships in the river dipped their colours.

"The wind freshened up to what used to be called a reef-topsail breeze. All I can say is that in her day she must have been a magnificent vessel to handle. She took not the slightest notice of a head-sea with a force six wind, and did exactly what she was told to do; hardly ever rolling or pitching.

"Our escort vessel signalled a farewell message, 'So long. Good luck. May you train many more hefty limbed young whelps.' The pier saluted as we passed: we dipped our ensign to acknowledge.

"The tow to the Bar Light vessel, seventeen miles from the Sloyne, took nine hours, nearly seven of which were against the flood tide, so that we could better keep her under control. Unlike the escort vessel and tugs, the Conway was perfectly steady. I doubt whether a pencil would have rolled off a table during the whole of the passage. This is entirely due to her deep bar keel. We averaged seven knots over the ground, from the Bar Light vessel to Puffin Island, where we stopped until nearly high water, when we took the Channel.

"This was uneventful, but the S bend in it, between No. 1 buoy and Beaumaris, required quick alterations in course with only two feet under our bottom. Under these conditions, the best method of towing the Conway is to shorten in the tow-ropes as much as possible, when she will answer immediately to any alteration in course. As the ship came around Gallows Point (about 1,000 yards S.W. Beaumaris) telegrams were sent to all cadets to rejoin the ship, to a summer term extended in August."

Captain Jim Thompson, Conway 1939-41, adds his memory of life in Conway.

"I was recalled early and we set about preparing Conway for the return of the cadets for the summer term. During this term we were advised that there was concern that Wales might be invaded by the Germans through Southern Ireland and so we were to be landed regularly at the Gazelle Slip and marched down to Beaumaris where we underwent firearm drill so as to repel any invasion! I left at the end of the term and within a week or so joined my first ship, the Tacoma Star, in West Float, Birkenhead. Fortunately I was transferred to a new ship loading in Queen's Dock, Glasgow a few days before the Tacoma Star sailed for she was lost with all hands that voyage and the cadet who had relieved me, another former Conway cadet, J. Benbow, lost his life along with all the others. 'But for the grace of God!'"

The new berth was close to that of H.M.S. Clio. She was another old wooden ship, a 22-gun corvette, sister to the well known Challenger of survey fame. She was built of African oak and launched from Sheerness as a screw vessel. Two of her commissions were served in the Pacific and she was paid off in 1874 to be loaned in 1876 to the Marine Society to replace the burnt out Warspite. Her last service commenced in 1877 when she was permanently lent to the North Wales, City of Chester and Border Counties Training Ship Society to be berthed off Bangor. The Clio catered for boys who were deemed to be without adequate means of support, education and control. She was certified for the accommodation of 260 boys between the ages of eleven and sixteen and for forty years she remained off Bangor. After sixty years afloat she went the way of all old ships and was sold and broken up on Bangor beach in 1920.

On Conway's arrival, the moorings were occupied by a Trinity House ship. The moorings were transferred, and by 8 a.m.on May 22nd, the Conway was secure in her new anchorage.

Chapter Fourteen

The Menai Straits

So at last the summer term began with 220 cadets on board. Water was
a problem as it was carried from the shore in buckets and large milk-
cans. The cadets had to pull three miles to Menai Bridge in the cutter
to get baths. The problem was solved when the big power water-boat of
Indefatigable was towed out of the Mersey and arrived off Bangor under
her own power. Other problems emerged. The playing fields were
much missed, the sight of so many ships in the Mersey had been
exciting for the lads, there was ever a shortage of food and the final
straw was the difficulty of getting and keeping a galley staff. Local
ladies helped by day in the galley and eventually they were replaced by
a Chinese group who lived on board.

One cadet recorded an amusing encounter. "I remember particularly
well during the summer term of 1941 that I was a member of the duty
cutter's crew, and as such was dressed in shorts and working rig. We had

gone to Bangor pier for provisions, etc., and while waiting about on the pier one of a pair of old ladies asked me what I was 'in' for. Puzzled, I asked what she meant; she asked what offence I had committed! The Conway was then blackened owing to the war and the ladies thought she was a reformatory."

War rig off Bangor Pier

The new anchorage proved to be very good for rowing and sailing. A sanatorium was established in the ground floor of a house, called Bryn Mel above the Gazelle slip in Anglesey and later the overflow of cadets was housed there. Games involved a two-mile trek to Beaumaris and an old gaol was used as a changing room. Later a fine field was found and some 150 cadets could be put ashore for games and a stable was adapted to become the new changing rooms. Naturally expeditions were made for the climbing of Snowdon. Life was different, but to keep in touch with the reality of the times parties of cadets were sent back to visit modern ships in Birkenhead.

"The Chinese cooks were provided by the Blue Funnel Line from the Merchant Navy Pool. Their cooking wasn't too bad - I doubt that

the best French chefs could have done any better with those·materials.
A few things I can remember about them:
The perpetual stink of rotten fish that hung outside the ship, port side
forward. They used to dry the fish and then pickle them - or
something! I never quite gathered how they ate it.
Their curry. I like hot curry but this was meant for someone with a
tougher mouth than I have!
Their expensive, gaudy shore-going clothes.
Their terrible temper. They were easily roused, and could be
dangerous."

"Seamanship with 'Hoppy' Lee was a favourite hour, as we really felt
that we were not at school, but sailors. You could hear the salt winds in
his voice when he spoke, and he rarely failed to make his lessons really
interesting, with little anecdotes of his own seafaring days. The penalty
for inattention in Mr. Lee's classes was invariably to write out Article 9
(Rule of the Road at Sea)."

Edmund Drew, Conway 1942-43, who became a Liverpool pilot and
long-standing friend, recalls memories from the letters he had sent
home. He discovered that, when his mother died, she had lovingly held
on to them and this enables us to read boyhood comments on life in
Conway. They are very much concerned with food parcels as every lad
was ever hungry. However, he seemed to have discovered a special
skill, vital for the survival of the young cadets.

"Thank you for the letter and parcel which I received on Friday.
That cake is very nice. I have one of the apples every night in my
hammock. The two cats had a fight; there is only one left now! No-one
has seen anything of the other for four days. There was a rat on the
lower deck yesterday and we were chasing it around. You can often
hear them squeaking on the orlop deck. They won't be able to poison
the rats here, because their bodies will make a terrible smell. They will
have to catch them.

"Thank you for the parcel. The apple tart is very nice, and so is the
cake. I like these cheese cakes. The cake was whole when I got it here

but the apple tart was just a big blob of apple and pastry in the middle of the plate. We never have anything to spread on the bread ... we were supposed to get our jam today.

"There are hundreds of rats hanging round. I was watching them running about while I was in my hammock the other night . They are not afraid of anyone at night.

"Thank you for the parcel, which I received yesterday. I was very hungry when I got it, because for the last few days they have only been giving us about five slices of bread a day. So far today we have had three slices. Usually I eat about eight or nine slices a day. Is there any shortage ashore? We are all going around like a lot of hungry dogs.

"Thank you for the rat trap. Last night I set it just behind my hammock. When I turned out this morning there was a great big black rat stuck in it. It measured over a foot long, including its tail. I expect to get sixpence for it. Two other fellows also caught one last night. I am going to set it in the same place tonight. Bread is the best bait and I had to throw the cheese over the side because it was smelling my chest out.

"Thank you for the parcel which I received yesterday. Since I wrote on Thursday I have caught two more rats, making a total of three ... or one and six pence! It is a fine trap and I scrub it after every rat I catch."

Reading these letters from young men in Conway it might be easy to forget that they were being prepared for a life at sea in wartime. Edmund Drew wrote this letter during his first trip to sea at the age if seventeen. The date is Sunday 23rd January, 1944 in the Atlantic.

"The other cadet and myself had been told to come on to the bridge at 4 o'clock in the afternoon, to watch the commodore for signals, write down messages being flashed to our ship or any other jobs to be done about the bridge.

"I was standing with the chief officer on the port side, when I noticed one of the escorting corvettes travelling at her fastest speed making as though to cut across our starboard bow. Suddenly she herself went hard over to starboard and I saw two black objects thrown into the air to land with splash in the water about five hundred yards from us. Immediately the chief officer said to me 'Tell the captain they are dropping depth charges.' As I ran into the wheel house I felt the whole ship give a violent shudder, and through one of the windows I saw a huge sheet of spray and foam rise out of the water, just astern of the escort. This was followed in turn by two more, and each time the ship gave a terrific shake for the depth charges were quite close. When I had informed the captain, the chief officer told the other fellow and myself to bend on two different halliards E flag and I flag. 'E' means 'emergency turn of 45 degrees to starboard' and 'I' means 'emergency turn of 45 degrees to port'.

"No sooner had we done this than there came from the commodore's ship two long blasts. All the ships in the convoy turned to port, and we ran up the I flag

"We could then see that two more of the escorts had joined the first, each flying from her yardarm a large, black pennant which means 'I am engaging an enemy submarine'. Many depth charges were being dropped, and we could see the water heave up, and then develop into a great pillar of white and then gently subside.

"By now the three ships were dropping astern, and had ceased depth charging but were lying still in the water as though listening intently for any movement far below the surface. The convoy, after making several more emergency turns, resumed its course, and we sighted land half an hour later. This occurred when we were within seven hours of Gibraltar, through which we passed in the dark. As far as we know the escort had no luck."

One can but reflect that lads of seventeen today might hardly understand how quickly their counterparts grew into men just over half a century ago and in their thousands were to die at sea. Some were even less than fifteen years old!

A good friend, Sid Davies, Conway 1942 - 43, adds to the story.

"Nearly three hundred young boys around fourteen or fifteen years crammed into the old 'wooden mother' as she was fondly refered to in the 'Conway Song'. Their possessions were housed in wooden chests ranged along the ship's side on the orlop deck and they slept in hammocks. Discipline was strict, with punishment by ropes-end meted out by cadet captains. Daily routine was conducted by bugle calls with knowledge of such calls being swiftly acquired to avoid the ropes-end, which hurried laggards along. The ship was divided into 'tops' as in naval ships under sail; the 'new chums' being divided between the Fo'csles - Port and Starboard, about thirty lads in each.

"Each 'top' was led by a Senior and Junior Cadet Captain, these being senior hands in their final terms before going to sea proper. Over these cadet captains the officers ruled, headed by Commander T.M. Goddard - fondly referred to as 'Wa-wa' because of his inability to pronounce his 'R's'. He and his wife and pretty daughter, Rosemary, occupied a third of the ship, his cabins had the ornate stern windows looking out over the moving waters. Under him was Lieutenant Commander 'Laurie' Lawrence, a genial rotund product of the R.N.'s lower deck who had made it to the higher ranks. 'Spooky', as Lieutenant Brooke-Smith was referred to, was a tall, bespectacled, well-liked executive officer who, although a strict disciplinarian, was respected for his impartial running of the daily routine. Under him were two single-stripers - 'Bossy Phelps', a cockney whose family were Thames watermen from generations past and who, with 'Tooley' Lee his counterpart was well liked. 'Tooley' was an army Warrant Officer who had been seconded to Conway to teach them the new-fangled unarmed combat!

"A headmaster fondly refered to as 'Bogbrush' (he had a shock of crinkly hair) and a motley bunch of teachers were non-residents who came from ashore each Monday to Friday to conduct lessons. Every known device was employed by the cadets to frustrate the teachers and it was reluctantly accepted by most that the educational achievements of the Conway were minimal and that the true value lay in the producing young men of spirit and initiative who would become the backbone of Britain's maritime industry.

"Wooden tables and stools occupied the Main Deck, each table sitting ten cadets with a cadet captain at the head. Sometimes there were 'seconds' and the messmen would rush back to their tables with a dish of potatoes, tip them smartly onto the bare table and hurtle back into the queue, hoping for more. The food was poor and sparse; we were given seagull eggs in season --they were strong and fishy. A liquid called 'skilly' was served - it seemed a cross between tea and weak coffee. On Sunday mornings we were given a piece of bacon at breakfast time - the piece was about three inches long. This with a piece of bread following porridge formed breakfast for ravenous mouths - we were permanently hungry.

"Seamanship was taught by 'Hoppy' Lee, so named because he had a false leg after an accident on board ship with a snapped wire hawser. He taught the intricacies of knots - bowlines and sheepshanks, timber hitches, carrick bends and so forth. He taught us how to rig a jury rudder, how to lay a kedge anchor and how to stow rice and grain and railway iron. We learnt that the stowage factor of coal was so many cubic feet to the ton, that grain and rice had to be ventilated properly and that mooring ropes had to be adjusted when working cargo. He taught us about 'handy-billies', 'single Spanish Burtons', and the mathematics of 'mechanical advantage' and the 'parallelogram of forces'. It was passed down to our class that we should ask 'Hoppy' the stowage factor of rhubarb and indeed one cadet called Mills was bold enough to put up his hand one day during a lesson on cargo stowage and asked 'What is the stowage factor of rhubarb, sir?' Sure enough old 'Hoppy' went berserk and lashed out with his book at the unfortunate Mills who lifted his arm to ward off the blows and was hounded out of the classroom. We never discovered why this question touched off such a reaction.

"Soon after joining the ship the 'new chums' would be introduced to clambering the main mast. A stout rope net was strung under it to catch anyone who might fall, but no one fell in my time. The climb at first was easy via the ratlines tied to the rigging but there was a large 'table' about fifty feet up and it was necessary to climb outwards over the 'futtocks' to gain this. Then a further climb would take one to another smaller 'table' forty feet higher and then another climb brought one right to the top of the mast and the 'truck' - the round wooden disk topping the mast. One or two intrepid cadets had been to sit on the 'truck'."

Other cadets take up the memories.

"The Outward Bound Sea School at Aberdovey was a popular break from the ship, for a whole month, (in the fourth term), thus chopping the term well up. On our return from this toughening-up course, we all felt real sailors. In my first couple of terms it was still reckoned great to walk out to the main yard-arm, along the top of the yard. This I myself once did, but my nerve failed me that I returned along the foot-rope.

"Young boys coming from their homes ... perhaps separated for the first time. Their welcome. Sitting in the cutter taking them to the ship, watched by twelve oarsmen - second termers and third ... who wore their top buttons undone and felt tough men of the world. The first question ... 'What's your name, chum? Where are you from?' Then someone cries, 'Look at his cap.' He gets on board. There is some welcome from his cadet captain. Then he must sweep the deck. He goes forward ... walks ... does not stop at an imaginary division ... unpardonable sin! 'Who gave you top?' Top? He does not know what it is ... but they tell him ... and perhaps he is made to stand on a chest and sing, and if he revolts then the wolves turn on him. I have seen it and I abhorred it. The cinema night comes ... a little excitement ... escape for a moment, but he must first pass an ordeal. Cadets descend into the hold where the film is shown, in order of seniority ... and they take the back seats. The juniors ... the new chums ... come last; and the horde is waiting ... the jeers ... the taunts, and someone will probably be made to sing. The jungle is waiting and the weaker arrive and try to slink to a seat as inconspicuously as possible. I know this makes people strong, but so does a prison camp.

"During my second term the war ended. In the evening we found out that the war had been won. A battery radio had been placed on one of the bollards on the main deck. I was on the main deck when the announcement was made. We were given forty-eight hours leave.

"The thing that impressed me most during my time on board was the Band! It was fine to see the members with their bugles shining and the white drum lanyards showing up against the black uniforms. The Conway band was twenty-one strong with fifteen bugles and five drummers and a new addition, the cymbals."

The move from the ship off Bangor to the shore-base at Plas Newydd was to have a profound effect upon the lives of the cadets. Captain Goddard put his thoughts on paper.

"I was instructed to search for such a place and eventually I visited the Marquess of Anglesey, two-thirds of whose house, Plas Newydd, was unoccupied since the United States Intelligence Corps had returned home soon after the end of the war. This part of the house, in wonderful condition, could accommodate 100 cadets and staff and provide excellent dining-rooms, kitchens, etc. The stables could be converted into classrooms ... there was a boat deck, sports pavilion, football fields and tennis courts.

"I wanted to know whether it was possible to take Conway through the Swellies, that dangerous stretch of water between the Menai Suspension and Tubular Bridges, and if so, was there anchorage with sufficient swinging room near to the house."

The Admiralty were unable to spare either a surveying vessel or officers so Captain Goddard undertook the task himself. He decided that with a thirty-one feet tide there would be two or three feet clearance from the bottom. Timing was important to negotiate the Swellies. To be safely towed through, she would have to be at the Menai Suspension bridge one hour twenty minutes before high water, at the beginning of the stand of the tide, and make the passage during the thirteen minutes it lasted. He also was sure that an anchorage was available near to Plas Newydd.

Captain Goddard descibed the tow:

"Now, everything being ready, I decided to make the passage on April 12th, 1949, when there was a thirty-one feet Liverpool tide. Unfortunately, a strong S.W. wind was blowing that day and after several fruitless attempts by the tugs to get heaving lines aboard, I decided it was too risky to make the passage. April 13th was a thirty-one feet six inches tide and a boisterous fresh wind blowing from the S.W., but I decided to go. I got under way two minutes late and this gave me twenty-eight to get to the bridge. I had previously instructed the pilot on the tug to do this part of the journey in half an hour. The tug took forty minutes and by the time I was under the bridge the ebb tide had commenced. However, the bridge did not obstruct my main truck, there being about three feet clearance, and I was soon abreast the Platters, where we altered course to close under the Caernarvonshire bank before hauling out again to pass between Price's Point and the Swelly Rock. These two negotiated safely, there was a four point turn to port to get her on to the. Tubular Bridge Beacon's transit. Unfortunately a squall on the port bow slowed the turn and the ebb tide took the ship towards the Goredd Island. I signalled the tug to head over to port but for five minutes we were towed alongside the island within five feet. However, we gradually got clear; at the beacon, before the Tubular bridge, we had got on the transit line, altered course for the centre of the south arch, passed under it with a good clearance, and then into deeper water. Conway was the deepest-draft vessel, twenty-two feet aft, and the largest, ever to have passed through the Swellies and I was glad when it was accomplished."

The two Liverpool tugs were the Dongarth, ahead, and the Minegarth abaft. Captain Goddard and fourteen lucky cadets were on board; and many thousands of thrilled spectators were on the Suspension Bridge and on the banks of the Straits. The ship had been in the dangerous mile between the two bridges for thirteen minutes.

Chapter Fifteen

Plas Newydd

For the Easter and summer terms in 1949 there were 275 cadets on board, the highest complement at that time in the history of the ship. Later the numbers would top 300. Changes were inevitable as all the new chums lived ashore but visited the ship for Sunday divisions and church. One cadet observed: "Moving from Plas Newydd to the ship was a grim procedure; we wondered how we should be received. In the end we enjoyed life better afloat than ashore, despite the open, draughty decks, the hammocks, and poor food."

Quickly two additional buildings were erected for the new entrants. The accomodation housed one hundred cadets and staff. The stables became the instruction block. Happily, the dock was dredged and put to excellent use. All was well.

Almost coinciding with the change in the anchorage of the ship, though entirely unrelated to it, there was to be a change of command. Captain

T.M. Goddard, R.N.R., had been appointed in 1934. He had been born in Rugby in 1888 and entered Conway as a cadet in 1905. During his time he had been captain of both the rugby and cricket teams. He started his sea career in 1907 and was to serve during the war in the armed liner Oceanic and with the Grand Fleet in H.M.S.Donegal. In 1919 he gained his extra-master (square-rigged) certificate together with the diploma of hydrographic surveying. Two years later he commanded the South African training ship 'General Botha', but within a year he helped in the start of the South African Navy with special duties in surveying the coast of Natal and Pondoland. Until 1931 he specialised in surveying the whole of the South West African coastline. When the South African Navy was disbanded in March 1934 it was provident that Captain Goddard was appointed to Conway in the July of that year.

Captain Goddard had the task of handling Conway during the difficult war years. During the bombing he slept at the after end of the main deck on a camp bed ... losing nights of sleep but always in command. The surveying of the sea-bed for the move from Bangor to Plas Newydd had been his responsibility. It was a job after his own heart ... careful, accurate and methodical. His Conway years had been truly remarkable.

A new staff-captain had been appointed when Captain T.M. Goddard retired at the end of the summer term in 1949. He was Captain Eric Hewitt, R.D., R.N.R. Captain Hewitt was also an old boy of Conway, 1919 -20, and took over the command.

The headmaster of the school was Wing Commander T.E.W. Browne, who had served during the First World War in the R.N.A.S and in the R.A.F., flying night bombers. During the Second World War he became a specialist navigator. He had joined the staff of Conway in 1934 and returned to the ship after his second time in the Royal Air Force.

Plas Newydd was ideally suited for training boys for the sea. It was on the north bank of the Straits with its own dock system, swimming pool and extensive playing fields. Above all it was in sight and easy reach of the Snowdonia range. The total complement was now a possible three hundred cadets. The plan was for the 'new chums' to spend their first two terms learning their 'trade' before being transferred to the ship.

The way ahead seemed well settled. Conway was 110 years old and fit to carry on the task and the new shore base was able to provide an even higher standard of training. On the ship's lower deck was framed her crest with its motto 'Quit Ye Like Men. Be Strong'

On Platters Ledge

In 1953 John Masefield concluded his revision of his book 'The Conway' just as the news of the loss of the ship was announced. He ended with these paragraphs.

"During last autumn, it was decided that she should lie at Bangor for the summer term, moving from Plas Newydd on the high tide of April 14th, and after the term she should go into dry-dock at Birkenhead for overhaul and refit, and tow back to Plas Newydd on the high tide of September. A ship of her size could not pass the Swellies save on those special tides.

"On Tuesday, April 14th, she slipped from her moorings, with two tugs Dongarth and Minegarth that had brought her to Plas Newydd four years before. She passed the Swellies and the Tubular Bridge without trouble. As she neared the Suspension Bridge, she was checked by the turn of a violent tide and a fairly fresh northerly wind. Under the strain, one of the towing lines parted, and the ship, that had taken a sheer to starboard, gently took the ground on the Caernarvonshire side, not far from the Suspension Bridge.

"She seemed, at first, to lie kindly, not seriously hurt, and well-supported along her whole length. Later, it would seem that with a turned tide her stern was slewed into deeper water and much damage done to her under body.

"By 5 a.m. on Wednesday, April 15th, it was clear that she was grieviously strained, with some beams gone and a visible hogging. Later in that day it was agreed that she should not be saved and must be declared a total loss."

To write about the Conway's grounding and her subsequent declared Constructive Total Loss is not easy. Captain Eric Hewitt had started the planning of the two-stage move for the dry docking in Birkenhead with the difficult passage through the Swellies in 1952. The old ship was to depend entirely upon the tugs as she had no engine power or steering gear or any anchors. Both Captain Hewitt and the Senior Menai Strait pilot had asked for three tugs but were over-ruled. The plan was to have five minutes in hand when they arrived at the Britannia Bridge at 0920 and the day, Tuesday 14th April 1953 opened with a light breeze, cloudless, fine and clear. The tide was expected to run at 4 knots and to make headway the tow was to be at 6 knots.

Moorings were slipped at 0815 and the tug Dongarth made fast forward with the tug Minegarth aft. The bow passed under the Britannia Bridge at 0923, three minutes late. However the fifteen minutes slack water did not occur and the west-going stream started at 0920. Pilot Jones aboard Conway asked for more power and realising that the vessel had only averaged two and half knots in twelve minutes and suggested that they should return stern first through the Swellies. Captain Hewitt decided against this advice and this was later accepted as correct ... going back was not possible. The vessel was then stationary in the water and the tug Minegarth at 1015 was ordered to let-go. The Minegarth joined the other tug forward and they attempted to tow in tandem. At some time between 1020 and 1030, at a position abreast Platters Rocks, an exceptionally strong tide eddy caused the Conway to take a violent sheer to starboard and she went ashore.

The Sub-Committee's unanimous decision was that Captain Hewitt and the entire team had acted with the highest standards of skill and seamanship. The conclusion was that the grounding was due to the exceptional condition of a 10 knot tide, when assessments had been made for a tide of 4 knots. There was nothing to be done.

Captain Hewitt felt this disaster very keenly. The memory never left him.

The committe of management in Liverpool, chaired by Lawrence Holt, faced the problem. Two hundred and fifty cadets were in training and the immediate reaction to the tragedy was to create a tented village. This was followed by a hutted camp. Life continued.

In September 1956 it was decided to dismantle the remains of the ship. The figure-head was rescued, together with a mast. The demand for mementoes was world-wide as the work continued. Disaster struck again on the 16th October when a workman's torch set the vessel alight. This was the end of a legend.

A new college was proposed and on August 1st, 1961 Mrs Hewitt laid the foundation stone. On the 6th May, 1964, the splendid buildings were opened by H.R.H. Prince Philip The rescued mast was erected at the southern end of the parade ground and the figurehead of Nelson at the northern end. Whilst the college was an era away from the previous environment, much effort was made to ensure that the routine resembled life aboard ship. Some things could not change. Queen Victoria had instituted the Queen's Gold Medal in 1866 for the 'finest sailor'. A short list of five was produced by the staff and all the cadets then voted for the recipient. This award was eventually to be taken over and presented to the best cadet in the Canadian Coast Guard Service and was known as the Queen's Conway Gold Medal. Sailing continued as a major enterprise and the gig races were well battled. There were also the annual rugby fixtures against Worcester and Pangbourne Nautical Colleges. Swimming in the outdoor pool in almost sub-zero temperatures was remarkably popular!

A royal visit

One visit that I made to Conway is well remembered by my family. It certainly was not the sermon that I delivered at the morning service! It was the large jug of fresh cream as we sat at table with Captain and Mrs Hewitt to enjoy an excellent lunch and listen to nautical tales. Children remember food.

Sadly, time was catching up as the shipping industry was changing rapidly. The demand for young officer cadets was falling and the majority of companies no longer supported Conway. Captain Hewitt retired in July 1968 and the end was inevitable.

Concrete Conway

The MMSA relinquished control of the school to the British Shipping Federation and the Cheshire County Council. By 1972 the number of cadets in training had fallen to the uneconomic level of 170 and the Cheshire Council gave notice that it wished to cease running Conway as a grant-aided school as from August 1974.

One hundred and fifteen years of nautical training were over. The final inspection was in June 1974 and the salute taken by the President of the Conway Club, Commodore David Smith, R.N. The ship was finally paid off on the 11th July, 1974.

Captain Hewitt reached the grand age of 91 and was in remarkable health. Sadly he died as the result of a fire in his home which he thought he had extinguished, only for it to ignite again after he had taken to his bed for the night. The Captain is still held in high regard by old Conways around the world. It truly is the end of an era.

The 3 ton carved teak figurehead of Lord Nelson was moved to the Royal Navy base in Portsmouth at the same time as it was changing its name from H.M.S Victory to H.M.S. Nelson. The Conway colours on 11th July 1974 were laid up in the Anglican Cathedral in Liverpool. The anchor was laid to rest in the Liverpool Maritime Museum. This school had provided thousands of officers for the Royal and Merchant Navies during its proud one hundred and fifteen years and produced four holders of the Victoria Cross and one George Cross and care has been taken to ensure that its memory is not to be obliterated by the passing years.

The Archbishop of Wales used these words when the colours were placed into the care of the Anglican Cathedral. 'The sum of the story is that the Conway has indeed taught the technical skills that we now take for granted in ships' officers. It has done more than that. The Conway has been concerned above all with the formation of character.'

H.M.S. Conway figure head

In the early 80's the Conway mast had been dismantled and had been put to one side. The Conway Club decided in 1989 that it should be refurbished and brought home to Birkenhead. It was in a bad condition. The Canadian Conways, in particular Mr. A. Sissons, Conway 1956 - 57, came to the rescue and three 50 foot long Douglas firs were shipped from Vancouver to Liverpool.

With skills that are almost lost, the repairs were effected under the guidance of shipwright Jimmy Gregory in the Cammell-Laird's Apprentice School, and the mast was assembled at the side of the old Egerton Dock in Birkenhead. A Conway stone was erected and a time capsule with the complete story was buried beneath it.

1859 H.M.S.CONWAY 1974
To the many thousands of Cadets Trained to Command
not forgetting those who lost their lives at sea.
'I must go down to the sea again
to the lonely Sea and the Sky'
John Masefield, OM, Conway 1891-94

On the 25th September 1993 there was a Service for the Blessing of the Mast as a symbol of the brotherhood of the sea and in memory of those who gave their lives. Never were the words of Psalm 107 more poignant.

'They that go down to the sea in ships, that do business in great waters; These see the works of the Lord, and his wonders in the deep.'

The last act of the story was the placing of the memorial and honour boards to rest in the St. Mary's Chapter House Scriptorium at Birkenhead Priory, now becoming known as the Conway Chapel. There could be no better home as the first Conway had been berthed nearby.

Conway will not be forgotten.

H.M.S. EAGLET

Chapter Sixteen

The Old Eagle

On the 1st of November, 1958, the Royal Naval Reserve and the Royal
Naval Volunteer Reserve were amalgamated into one organisation to be
known as the Royal Naval Reserve. This is part of the waterfront story
in Merseyside and my contact as a Padre involved over thirty years of
work in H.M.S. Eaglet and friendships with the men and women of the
R.N.R. It is one of the finest 'clubs' in the world ... and I was proud to
become Eaglet's Chaplain in 1966.

The Eagle, as she was then called, was built at Northfleet on the Thames, a wooden 74 gun ship of the Third Rate. Eagle was launched in February, 1804, and was destroyed by fire in 1927. She saw 123 years of service and for 64 years was home of both Reserves on Merseyside.

Until the middle 19th century the ships of the Royal Navy were classified by Rate. Eagle was a Third Rate. This system had originally been based upon the rates of pay to which captains of warships had been entitled according to the sizes of the vessels which they commanded. In course of time this system came to refer to the number of guns which these vessels carried. A First Rate mounted between 100 and 120 guns, the Rate decreasing with the lesser number of guns mounted, until the lowest Rated ships were the Sixth Rate frigates of 20 to 28 guns. Most vessels of the day were seventy-four gun ships, ideal for the work of patrolling and relatively easy to handle.

Fitted for sea at Woolwich Dockyard, she was commissioned for service in the Channel Fleet. The first entry in her log is dated 16th March, 1804. The next day, according to the official notes, she 'hoisted the flag of Rear-Admiral Thornborough, who came aboard with his retinue.'

In 1810 she was employed at Cadiz, on the Mediterranean Station, and in the Gulf of Venice until 1814, after which she returned to Chatham and was paid off. Then she was laid up until 1844. During that time she was cut down to a frigate and treated as a Fourth Rate of 50 guns. Re-commissioned at Chatham she served off the South East coast of South America, the West Indies and on the Mediterranean Station. She returned to England in February, 1848, and was paid off at Devonport where she remained in reserve until 1856. She was fitted for Coast Guard Service and was stationed at Falmouth until 1858 and then at Milford Haven. Finaly she returned to Portsmouth and was paid off.

She was next fitted as a training ship, and stationed in Southhampton Water in November, 1860, where she remained until March, 1862, when she again returned to Portsmouth to be paid off. She was then fitted for an R.N.R. drill ship at the port of Liverpool, where she arrived in June, 1862.

During her service afloat, the Eagle wore an admiral's flag three times. She was flagship at the Texel in 1804, again on the South East Coast of America Station in 1844 and yet again seventy years later when she became flagship in Liverpool between 1914 and 1919. She was never involved in action, but gave sterling service to the Royal Navy.

During her service, Eagle's complement had been about 600 men. Her officers were the captain and five lieutenants, a master and his mate and a lieutenant of marines. The Marine detachment consisted of about ninety scarlet-coated rank and file. The non-service officers were the surgeon and his assistant, the chaplain and the purser ... these gentlemen carried no rank.

The old Eagle

Originally, her seamen ratings numbered some 556 men and thirty boys exclusive of officers' servants and 'widows' men'. These latter were non-existent and in theory amounted to 1% of the actual crew. The books of Eagle carried about six as her share of these mythical sailors, whose pay and allowances, by very old naval custom, provided a fund to pay pensions to the widows of officers. These fictitious 'men' continued to be borne on the books of H.M. Ships until about 1830 and their rate of pay was that of an able seamen. Nelson's 'blind eye' was put to good use and must have saved much paper work and bureaucracy.

The Fleet Reserve was instituted in 1852 and continuous service in the Navy in the following year. Obviously it was finally realised that there would be a dearth of trained seamen in the Navy for some years, and particularly in time of war. Permanent service was a new idea.

Recruitment of merchant seamen into the Royal Naval Reserve commenced in 1861 and officers in the merchant service were first offered commissions in the following year. Times change and today there are no merchant ratings in the R.N.R., although the officers remain. To train these newcomers in the ways of the Navy, three drill-ships were established - in London, North Shields and Liverpool. So commenced the long association of Her Majesty's Ship Eagle, the Naval Volunteers and the port of Liverpool. The first Liverpool drill-ship was the old warship Hastings which had been District Ship of the Liverpool Coast Guard District, but she did not remain long here and departed for Queenstown upon the arrival of her successor, Eagle.

The story of H.M.S. Eagle has been written by John Smart and Edward Jones and was presented as a paper on the 13th November, 1958, to the Liverpool Nautical Research Society. I was privileged to be the President of that illustrious Society for a number of years and have received permission to recall some details from that paper.

"The drill-ship Eagle arrived from Spithead in tow of H.M. paddle sloop Geyser at 4.40 a.m. on Sunday, June 29th 1862. In the excitement of reporting the fraternal conflict between Confederates and Federals, Monday's paper overlooked any mention of her arrival, but a few days later she took up her berth in the north-east corner of the old Queen's Dock. In those days the layout of the docks in that area differed considerably from that which now prevails. Entrance was by means of the Queen's Basin leading into Queen's Dock. King's Dock, much smaller than the present dock, was entered by a short passage on the north side of the Basin. Despite her having been in Liverpool for over sixty years, very little information is available with regard to the ship or her berths. One supposes that being such a familiar feature of the dockland of her day she was taken very much for granted.

"The Royal Naval Reserve continued to drill aboard her until 1911, her Captain carried he rank of a Commander, R.N. Between 1862 and 1908 this appointment was held in succession by nineteen officers, and she had the honour of claiming that, of all the R.N.R. centres in operation in 1898, those of Liverpool and Stornoway had trained a number of men far in excess of any others in the country.

"The Royal Naval Volunteer Reserve may be said to be descended from the Royal Naval Artillery Volunteers. Hitherto, such volunteers as had been available were professional seamen, but the R.N.A.V. opened enlistment to young civilians who were interested in matters naval. The Liverpool Corps of the R.N.A.V. was formed in 1873 with headquarters in H.M.S. Eagle. Each Corps was composed of two or three batteries, each consisting of a sub-lieutenant, a chief petty officer, 1st and 2nd class petty officers and from fifty to seventy gunners. The combined Liverpool and Southport Corps united to form the Liverpool Brigade in 1876. A brigade comprised from four to six batteries with an establishment of about 450 men.

"The volunteer gunners were intensely enthusiastic and at its zenith the Brigade had units in Liverpool, Southport, Bangor, Caernarfon and Birkenhead. By this time Eagle had changed berth from Queen's to King's Dock and in the 1880's lay at what is now the berth of the Booth Steam Ship Company at North 2 King's Dock. Unfortunately, as had happened with the Sea Fencibles (men recruited for the defence of U.K. only and dating back to Nelson's time) and again with the Royal Naval

Coast Volunteers (started in 1853), official encouragement was lacking. The guns were vintage pieces, the gear scanty and there was little or no provision for sea training. In effect the gunners were soldiers dressed as seamen. An interesting feature of the uniform was that the blue jean collars had waved tapes, the officers' silver stripes were waved and both these features were revived in later years upon the formation of the R.N.V.R. The waved lace, in gold instead of silver, continued to distinguish R.N.V.R officers until recently replaced by the regular pattern, but can still be seen upon the sleeves of officers of the Sea Cadet Corps.

"In 1892 the Admiralty who, in truth to tell, had never cared for anything less than the genuine article, saw fit to disband these eager young men and today an In Memoriam notice preserved aboard H.M.S. Eagle proclaims that the R.N.A.V., 'Died of Neglect'.

"In view of the volunteer spirit so evident in the latter half of the last century, it is indeed strange that the Board of Admiralty were not as ready as the War Office to direct it into useful channels. Even the formation of the R.N.V.R. in June 1903 was accepted somewhat sceptically by authority and not with the enthusiasm which its sponsors had expected. Tradition has it that the first enrolment into the Mersey Division of the R.N.V.R. took place on board H.M.S. Eagle in King's Dock on New Year's Day 1904. The target of 300 men was very soon reached and the first drills were held on board the old ship on the 8th March. It was then a few days over 100 years since she had been launched, and her appearance was such that her three admirals would have not recognised this Noah's Ark-like structure as a once proud seventy-four gun sailing ship of the line."

The Royal Naval Reserve (officers and men serving in the mercantile marine) had continued to use the Eagle as a drill-ship for forty-one years, but forsook her in 1903. In that year was introduced a more realistic scheme of training in sea-going cruisers, but this only lasted for two years and in 1905 the R.N.R. returned to the Eagle. In the meantime, owing to the proposed rebuilding of King's and Queen's

Docks, she had been moved to the north side of Salthouse Dock in 1904. When the R.N.R. re-occupied the ship in 1905 the R.N.V.R. moved across to the Custom House in Canning Place and although that grim pile lacked the naval atmosphere, it had at least one advantage. The drill hall was in the north-east corner of the building and was large enough to accommodate the whole of the Division when mustered for drill and inspection.

"On the 31st March, 1911, the R.N.R. vacated Eagle and she was turned over to the R.N.V.R. for their sole use. The Division comprised seven companies of 100 officers and men, four at Liverpool, two outlying companies at Birkenhead and one in Southport. They were not however to enjoy possession for very long.

"International events were moving to a gigantic climax which, among its lesser results was to embroil even the centenarian Eagle. Shortly after the outbreak of war she was once again on active service, although in a stationary capacity. Captain H. H. Stileman was appointed to her as Senior Officer, Liverpool, and upon the 2nd of November, 1914, he received his flag. Thus once again, and for the third time in her long and somewhat chequered career, she became a flagship. This duty she performed for the duration of the war."

Edward Jones continued his thoughts as he recalled his own observations on H.M.S. Eagle during his time aboard during the first World War.

"On the lower deck, in the orlop, were the cells, very dark and small and not at all inviting. In the early hours of a cold February morning the alarm was raised. A prisoner had escaped from his cell. The guards were called out and stationed at all exits, but upon examination it was found that he had gone out by removing the bars from the port in the cell and dropped into the dock with the aid of his blanket and dare not let go. The water was perishing cold and it was freezing hard. He was told to come on board but with chattering teeth he answered, 'I c-c-can't, there's no foothold. I can't hold on much longer.' He was unable to obtain a foothold owing to the turn of the bilge and a rope was lowered to him, but he was so cold that he dare not let go of the blanket to tie the rope around his waist. He shouted, 'I can't come up' then a vast voice from out of the darkness shouted, 'Come up, or I shoot'. Eventually a dinghy was lowered and he was picked up more dead than alive, a very sorry man.

"In one of the breast-hooks or stringers on the port side was cut: Built by Sir Wm. Rule at Northfleet in 1804, 74 guns,1723 tons. This particular beam was fifteen inches square and it was amazing how the frames and diagonals were fitted together in the forepeak. Above the quarter-deck was the figurehead but unfortunately it was in a dark place and could easily be missed. I believe that the ship's wheel was aboard somewhere but I never saw this. The handrails of the companion-way leading down to the wardroom were covered with coachwhipping complete with turk's head and stopper knots, a beautiful piece of work.

"The old boatswain was always pleased to get someone interested and give them a few lessons in passing the ball to and fro. Very interesting, but very tedious. He was quite a character, that old bosun. When he piped, 'Everyone aft!', he would stand at the top of the midship companion and say: 'Come on, my dears, come along, my dears. Come along, gentlemen, come on you scallywags. Come on, you lazy louts', and many other terms of endearment followed if we were slow enough to hear them.

"In the wardroom on the sideboard stood a beautiful model of a seventy-four in bronze, complete with guns, anchors, cables, masts, yards and all the details. It stood on a four-wheeled carriage and I admired it many times. I wonder what became of it?"

Eagle continued as the base ship in Liverpool throughout the war, as accommodation for ratings in transit. During this time there was little if any contact with the R.N.V.R.

At the start of the First World War, a battleship called the Almirante Cochran was being built by Armstrong, Whitworth and Co., Ltd., for the

Chilean Navy. Work had stopped until 1917 when she was purchased by the British Government. She was redesigned as an aircraft carrier and destined to be called Eagle. When the carrier was launched on the 8th June, 1918, our old friend, the Eagle, was renamed Eaglet.

The Eaglet continued as the base ship in Liverpool for the rest of the war, mainly for the accommodation of ratings in transit. There was little connection with the R.N.V.R. as such. When the war had started in 1914, some R.N.V.R. officers and ratings had been drafted for sea service, but by far the majority were mustered into Naval Brigades and, for some obscure reason, were turned into soldiers! The Brigades were sent into Antwerp in an attempt to stem the German invasion and those not captured or interned were later reorganised into the Royal Naval Division, which served at Gallipoli and on the Western Front, winning undying fame at Vimy Ridge, Passchendale and Cambrai. The Brigades were disbanded after the armistice.

Chapter Seventeen

The W.R.N.S.

Mention must be made of the formation of the W.R.N.S. On the 26th November, 1917, the First Lord of the Admiralty, Sir Eric Geddes, submitted a letter to his Sovereign, King George V, and it started with these words:

"Sir Eric Geddes, with his humble duty, begs to inform Your Majesty that the Board of Admiralty have under consideration the possibility of substituting women for men." Those brave words marked the beginning of the Women's Royal Naval Service and two days later the King pencilled his approval to the document.

The start of the Service in Liverpool was the appointment of a Director of Wrens and she received an instruction 'Appoint eight W.R.N.S. on attachment to Eaglet and secure accommodation.' That was the 8th January, 1918. True to form she received a further cable on the 16th January 'Cancel attachment'.

However, the Liverpool Wrens did get under way as the rather tired photograph of Eaglet's Division reveals. Liverpool was the last of the original Divisions and started in March 1918 and the appearance of the first two W.R.N.S. Officers in uniform caused great excitement. The civilian women employed by the Naval authority were initially reluctant to be enrolled. The work was mostly clerical with telephone operators and drivers. Two officers were seconded to Holyhead for de-coding duties. Others were employed at the Royal Naval Air Stations at Walney Island and Llangefni in Anglesey where they worked as cooks, stewards and in general duties.

W.R.N.S. Logo

Each Wren was given a pocket book with a paper to be considered as 'confidential'. It was signed by Katherine Furse, the first Director of the W.R.N.S. The content was surely pertinent to the times.

"You are being entrusted with the Honour of working for your Country and, as a member of the Women's Royal Naval Service, you must do your Duty in a serious and generous spirit.

"The Navy is the Senior Service, and we must proudly maintain its Reputation and prove worthy of its best Traditions as well as of the confidence now placed in us.

"Officers, Subordinate Officers and Women of the W.R.N.S. must unite in friendship, trust and kindness. Let us, by our courtesy, sincerity of purpose and understanding of mutual difficulties, bind our Service together with a bond of Loyalty to our King and Empire.

"Discipline is a necessity in a Service such as ours, but let it be obtained as 'in Honour bound' and not by penalties. If we can produce the Right Spirit we need have no fear of restrictions or punishments because each single one of us will be led to a greater effort for the good name of the 'Wrens'.

"No Work is menial or unworthy of any individual if it be undertaken with zeal and alacrity. We must share each other's toil and never hesitate to help where help is needed. We all know that it is merely our duty to carry through our individual task, and we shall need no reminder of this when we remember for ourselves what we are working for. Self-discipline leads to the greater discipline of the whole, so each one of us can contribute our mite to the Great Ideal.

"Let us always show Friendliness and Sympathy to our Sister Services of the Army and of the Air Force, only by kindly competition in Efficiency and games to obtain supremacy for the W.R.N.S.

"As we all look for and depend on our Welcome from one another now, so let us extend it to all who join us in the future, putting aside all prejudice and remembering only that as women we are united in the W.R.N.S. to help our Country, the Navy and each other.

KATHERINE FURSE

Director,
W.R.N.S."

1918

The following prayer was included with that citation.

"Consider NELSON'S Prayer :-

"May the Great God whom I worship Grant to my Country and for the benefit of Europe in General a great and Glorious Victory, and may no misconduct in anyone Tarnish it; and may humanity after Victory be the predominant feature in the British Fleet. For myself individually I commit my life to Him, Who made me and may His Blessing light upon my endeavours for serving my Country faithfully. To Him I resign myself and the just cause which is entrusted me to Defend. AMEN, AMEN, AMEN.

"The last entry in Nelson's Diary, written on board H.M.S.Victory on the morning of the Battle of Trafalgar, Monday, 21st October, 1805:-

Remember the Empire expects that every woman will do her duty.
Fear God
Honour the King."

Eaglet 1918

On 18th September, 1919, the Director of the W.R.N.S. received a letter from Their Lordships expressing appreciation for the Wrens' contribution to the war effort. The branch was demobilised.

In October 1935, a Sub-Committee of the Imperial Defence considered the question of the creation of a Women's Reserve and in May 1936 reported: 'Women's Reserve deemed not desirable'. Dame Katherine Furse responded the following year by writing to the Board of Admiralty offering the Association of Wrens in the event of an emergency. This was not ignored and a Paper was submitted on 22nd November, 1938 proposing the reformation of the W.R.N.S. Early in 1939 Mrs Vera Laughton Matthews was appointed Director of the W.R.N.S. and by the end of that year the strength reached 3,000.

The peak number was reached in September, 1944, when there were 74,635 officers and ratings in 90 categories and 50 branches. Towards the end of the conflict the Director used these remarkable words at the conclusion of a speech:
'Our lives are going to be wider and deeper because of all that we have learnt in the Service. And when peace comes you will take your place in civilian life to such good purpose that people will say, "Well, you see, she was a Wren!" '

The work of the Wrens continued after the war and expanded. This was acknowledged on the 8th April, 1974 when the W.R.N.S. Regulations became obsolete and the Branch came under the Naval Discipline Act for the first time. Much more was to follow and the Geddes's statement of 1917 that there should be consideration of 'the possibility of substituting women for men' truly belongs to another century. It actually happened. I received an e-mail as follows.
"Subject: Demise of W.R.N.S.
The W.R.N.S. was subsumed into the R.N. on 1 November, 1993."

Chapter Eighteen
The Eaglet

By the end of the First World War with her new name, Eaglet, she was in serious disrepair. Gone was the familiar white streak broken by her gun-ports and her black hull had been repainted in standard navy grey. What remained of her masts had at some time been cut down to the level of the roof ridge over the upper deck, and she looked more like Noah's Ark than ever.

In 1921 the Mersey Division of the R.N.V.R. was reformed with a strength of 400 men under the command of Commander William Maples, R.N.V.R. The composition of the Division was by companies, each 100 strong, of which numbers one, two, three and seven paraded in the ship at Salthouse Dock. Number four company was located at Southport, number five mustered at Caernarfon and number six in Birkenhead. In 1922 the Southport company was disbanded but in

September, 1923, a new Sub-Division came into being in Manchester. For its accommodation the war-time sloop H.M.S. Sir Bevis, now re-named Irwell, was berthed in Fairbrother Street Wharf, Salford. The local wits referred to her as H.M.S. Neverbudge.

John Smart and Edward Jones continued their memoirs.

"By 1926 the old Eaglet, which had now been afloat for almost a century and a quarter, was deemed to be unfit for further service and was ordered to be paid off for disposal. It was originally intended to replace her by H.M.S. Goole, a war-time minesweeper, but the Goole was too small for this duty and was transferred to Manchester. In August, 1926, all three drill-ships, the Irwell (the war-time sloop) on the west side and the Eaglet with the Goole alongside, lay in Salthouse Dock together for a short time, a unique occasion. Without going into too much detail regarding the change-over, the Irwell (ex H.M.S Sir Bevis) from Manchester became the present Eaglet and the Eaglet-designate, late the Goole, became the Irwell which we know today (1959).

H.M.S. Eaglet in Salthouse Dock, 1922

"A farewell banquet had been held aboard the old veteran on the 2nd of June and upon the evening of Thursday, the 2nd of September, 1926, the Division was mustered aft and at eight bells, as the notes of the Last Post echoed across the quiet dock, her ensign was slowly lowered for the last time and her service as one of the King's ships was ended. She had served under a queen and five kings in the 126 years which had elapsed since Sir William Rule designed her. Her ship's company marched away to the new ship and she was left, silent and deserted as she had been left so frequently before. Again the bugles rang out across the still waters, signalmen aboard the new Eaglet hoisted her ensign and the change-over was completed."

The old Eaglet left Liverpool one misty morning in the following February and was towed to Mostyn, where she was beached preparatory to the difficult task of taking apart her aged timbers. On the 19th of April she caught fire as she lay and was burnt out. Her epitaph is contained in a few pages of verse preserved aboard her successor.

'Now not a vestige of her remains,
the old ship has gone for good
To some special Valhalla for seventy-fours
and the ships which were built of wood.'

The old ship's magnificent figurehead, a bearded and helmeted warrior, her wheel and an original door and door-frame still remain intact today in the shore-based Eaglet.

During the Second World War, officers and men of the Mersey Division mobilised for service with the Royal Navy; 120 lost their lives in the conflict.

H.M.S. Eaglet was commissioned (1941 - 1945) as Base Ship Liverpool wearing the flag of Commander-in-Chief Western Approaches, Admiral Sir Percy Noble and then Admiral Sir Max Horton.

An excellent book entitled 'The Sea Chaplains' by the Reverend Gordon Taylor, a wartime chaplain himself and the R.N.R. chaplain of the

London Division until 1970, includes a section of especial interest to Merseysiders.

"In September 1939 the Royal Navy began its blockade of Germany in Northern waters by using the older cruisers to cover the exits to the Atlantic, the Denmark Strait and the Faeroe Islands Passage. In the October the ships were augmented by the first of the liners which had been converted into armed merchant cruisers (A.M.Cs).

"In February 1940 twenty A.M.Cs. were on the Northern Patrol, four were with the Halifax Escort Force and twelve were in the Mediterranean.

"A chaplain for the A.M.Cs. was appointed in August 1940 in order to minister to the men who had the arduous work of the Northern Patrol, and he was a particularly good choice. He was Eric Evans R.N.V.R., then Vicar of Crossens, near Southport, Lancashire, who for five years before the war had been the Senior Chaplain of the Mersey Mission to Seamen, and who therefore knew well many of the merchant service officers and men who were serving under the T.124 (or T124x) Agreement. Such to a large degree were the ships' companies of the A.M.Cs., though their captains and commanders were generally Royal Navy officers who had been brought back from fairly recent retirement and a considerable proportion of the seamen were also from the Royal Navy.

"Evans made his first patrol in the former Bibby liner Cheshire, and followed this with others in the former P. & O. Chitral, the former Anchor liners Cilicia and Circassia, and the Wolfe, which was the former Canadian Pacific Montcalm as renamed. He remembers spending Christmas 1940 in northern waters. From early in 1941 he worked from the base at Halifax (Seaborn) on a roving commission with the A.M.Cs. of the Western Patrol, before returning to Britain in the former Cunarder Alaunia.

"As Evans' ships in the North Atlantic reduced in number, his suitability for work in such ships was again recognised by his appointment in October 1941 to the base-ship which was anchored permanently at Freetown, Sierra Leone, the very old former Union-

Castle liner Edinburgh Castle, for sea-going duty with the A.M.Cs. operating in the South Atlantic in the South American Division. "He joined the former Union-Castle liner Carnarvon Castle and stayed in her at the captain's request until March 1942 when he took passage to Cape Town to join, first the former Furness Withy liner Queen of Bermuda and the former Royal Mail Alcantara. After almost three years in A.M.Cs. he returned home to Britain and in due course joined the cruiser Bermuda, which became engaged in Russian convoy work. He ended his service on the staff of the admiral at Bombay. Few clergy who joined the Navy as Temporary Chaplains, R.N.V.R., can have seen more sea-time then Eric Evans. After all his voyaging he returned to parochial life in West Lancashire, and saw many arduous years as Rector of North Meols and Archdeacon of Warrington. He died on 25th of December 1977."

When I arrived on Merseyside in 1961, Eric was a member of the Mersey Mission to Seamen's committee. He never talked about his wartime adventures, but proved to be a mine of information and a loyal friend.

Sometimes memories are brushed down and given an airing. Happily as the years passed, I joined the 'old and bold' on many festive occasions, when anecdotes were spun out to amuse and little was made of the suffering and hardship of wartime at sea. Eaglet was a great meeting place for 'swinging the lamp' and telling the tale.

After World War II the Mersey Division was reformed under Commander, later Captain E.N. Wood, D.S.C., V.R.D., R.N.R.. A minesweeper was attached to the Division in 1947 as Sea Training Tender and named H.M.S. Mersey. She was to be replaced a number of times.

Richard Whittington-Egan in his collection of articles entitled 'Liverpool Roundabout' has recorded a visit to Eaglet in 1957.

"Wavy Navy Occasion"
"We sat around the beautifully-polished table in the creaking ward-

room, a dozen of us - bank clerks, barristers, engineers, directors of city firms, dentists and doctors, spare time sailors fled for an hour or two from the limited horizons of office, court and consulting room to the wider seascape of lunch afloat aboard H.M.S. Eaglet in the Salthouse Dock.

"Above us on the wall, discreetly framed in sober oak, the ensign of our common denominator, a fragment of smooth blue sleeve bearing the zigzag golden circle of the wavy navy. Since 1951 that 48-year-old badge has become a museum piece, for nowadays the officers of the R.N.V.R. sport rings regular as those of their straight-laced brethren of the Royal Navy. But sailors thrive on tradition, and to commemorate the old distinction the officers of the Mersey Division surrendered their discarded ranks to the melting-pot, 100.20 ounces troy of lace (you must not call it braid) which yielded 1.76 ounces of fine gold and 70.45 ounces of fine silver, totally valued at £45. 10s. This salvaged splendour was made into a gold-plated silver plaque which, surrounding that historic sleeve, now gleams magnificently upon the ward-room bulkhead.

"Three times a week on average they foregather for this convivial midday occasion, the members of the wardroom, but in the evenings it is a different matter. Then, there is work to be done. The onerous work of training close on a thousand men and women in the craft of seamanship.

"After lunch I did a tour of the ship and saw for myself the class-rooms of this floating school. There were rooms - or should it be cabins? - full of benches of complex mechanical apparatus, where lectures on gunnery and wireless and radar maintenance and procedure are delivered. There was a place that looked rather like the reporters' room in a newspaper office. 'We teach them how to type here,' said the petty officer in charge nodding at the rows and rows of canopied typewriters. 'Pencils are out in the modern navy, wireless operators are trained to type all messages direct as they come in in morse.' Remembering my own futile attempts to master morse in wartime I registered suitable admiration for the versatility of the modern matelot.

"A few steps further for'ard was a gruesome room dedicated to the training of sick-berth attendants, where in glass cases glinted batteries of shining needles and trays of terrifying silver surgical instruments; and here too was a genuine, though disarticulated, human skeleton in a glass fronted cupboard. Around the walls hung numbers of temperature charts and various sick-forms and reports, all neatly completed with a wealth of hair-raising detail. From these I learned, with regret, that A.B. Fanackapan, Fred, was suffering from lobal pneumonia, enteric fever and malaria, whilst his shipmate, Joe Muggins, was down with T.B. Seeking to escape from so disturbing a local (like Mr. Somerset Maugham I should infinitely prefer locale, but the O.E.D. forbids), I dashed through an open doorway right into a fully-equipped dental surgery!

"Being distinctly allergic to dentistry in any of its manifestations I had to be revived with excellent sherry in the ward-room. There, a pleasant chubby-faced officer asked me how long I had been in the 'Andrew' and I gave myself away for the landlubber that I am by admitting that I had never heard of Andrew Miller, the formidable leader of a particularly successful press-gang, whose name has come to mean, in naval parlance, the navy.

"Nor did I know that 'Fanny Adams' was the sailor's name for tinned mutton, so christened by Jolly Jack in dubious tribute to the victim of a peculiarly gory murder of the 1860's.

"Thus exposed, I felt it was high time to abandon ship, but after all I had seen I walked down the gang-plank with the feeling that the R.N.V.R. in Liverpool is certainly living up to the motto which is painted conspicuously across a beam that spans the Eaglet's drill hall. 'Si vis pace para bellum' it says, which a superior rating obligingly translated for me as 'If you want peace prepare for war' "

Incidentally, this article by Whittington-Egan was written under a sub-heading: 'The table talk of one who though not in the Andrew enjoyed its hospitality and mercifully missed eating sweet Fanny Adams for lunch.'

The R.N.V.R. wavy stripes were replaced by straight stripes with 'R' in curl in 1952. In the same year the W.R.N.R. was formed. In 1958 the R.N.V.R. was amalgamated into a new unified Royal Naval Reserve.

I joined the Division as Chaplain in 1966, having been an Officiating Royal Navy Chaplain since 1961 and retired from the R.N.R. in 1981. I started my ministry with the Mersey Mission to Seamen in 1961 and eventually retired in 1989. Before all this nautical activity, I had served in wartime as Royal Air Force pilot and then a number of years as a Padre with the Air Training Corps. The sea and the air have much in common … both command respect and bind men into a remarkable fellowship.

My memories of the 'floating hulk' are fond, but distant. The first duty of the Chaplain on Drill Night in Eaglet was to conduct prayers at Divisions. The drill deck was large and decidedly ill-lit. With the full ship's company assembled after much shuffling and restrained shouting, the order came ... 'Off caps'. Forward I went and for two minutes or so the stage was mine. It was a challenge. Quickly I realised that a piece from the Liverpool Echo was more likely to grab their attention than Cranmer's best prose. I knew that I had communicated when during my tour of the ship, my leg was pulled and the topic dissected. There was one bit of Cranmerian prose that never failed. Too often the lights invariably dimmed from fatigue and old-age. That was the cue for me to make use of the Evensong Collect, 'Lighten our darkness we beseech Thee, O Lord ...' and there was always a fervent 'Amen'.

Chapter Nineteen

The Shore Base

When in 1972 the old ship was declared redundant and we moved to the new shore Headquarters in Princes Dock, the official opening on the 2nd May was conducted by Vice Admiral Sir Gilbert Stephenson, K.B.E., C.B., C.M.G. The Service took place in the Cathedral and from that distance I read the Dedication Prayer for the new Eaglet. The ship's company marched proudly through the City to our new home.

I had first met Vice-Admiral Stephenson (nicknamed with affection 'Monkey') when I attended for the first time as ship's chaplain the Annual Battle of Atlantic Service in our Cathedral. At the outbreak of the Second World War the Admiral had been recalled from retirement, even though he was seventy years of age. He was sent to Tobermory on the Isle of Mull on the west coast of Scotland.

Here the various groups did their final warm-ups before tackling the North Atlantic, the convoys and the hunting packs of U-boats. As the majority of each ship's company was 'hostilities only', they had to be given a quick, sharp shock, if they were to survive. Trades had to be mastered in weeks and months, not in years as in the peace-time Navy. 'Monkey' Stephenson was the man chosen to put the fear of God into the final training at Tobermory.

A story, which probably has gone the rounds as long as there have been Navies, has also been attributed to him. He would board a ship unannounced, at an impossible hour, and create havoc. The legendary story is that on one such occasion, 'Monkey' placed his cap on the deck and indicated to a passing matelot, 'That's a bomb!' Naturally, the quick thinking lad promptly booted it over the side. The Admiral did not flinch, announced 'Man overboard!' and started his stop-watch.

Another such tale tells of the Admiral climbing over the side in the small hours and, having made his way to the bridge without being accosted, pressed the alarm button. Nothing happened. Not a soul appeared. Nothing! Eventually a dishevelled engineer stuck his head around the door and announced, 'If you keep pressing that so-and-so button, you'll flatten the so-and-so battery!' The Admiral's response has not been recorded.

The first shore base

So it was that I met the Admiral for the first time at the back-end of the Cathedral at the start of the Battle of Atlantic Service. There he stood, five feet tall with his ceremonial sword tucked in like a crutch, as it almost dragged the ground. He strode towards me.

'Who are you?'

'Evans, sir, Chaplain Superintendent of the Mersey Mission to Seamen.' That did not seem to impress him one little bit. He gave a sort of a grunt.

'Are you any good?'

I knew that this was the moment which had faced many a young officer in Tobermory. If I showed humility, he would have kicked me over the side. I was amazed to hear my instinctive reply to his challenge.

'Yes, sir, I'm the right man for the job!'

'Quite right, my boy, shouldn't do it , if you weren't!'

No wonder decades before, the men were relieved to escape from Tobermory to face the dangers of the North Atlantic storms and U-boats. He smiled. Gave a nod of approval and stumped off to his place in the procession. This was the 'Terror of Tobermory', then in his nineties!

The ship's company, following the Service in the Cathedral, marched through the City to the new Eaglet. The building was system-built and largely prefabricated. Back at our new headquarters, on the edge of the Mersey, we all lined up on the quayside. 'Monkey' mounted the dais, so that we might see him, and switched off the bank of microphones. He ordered us to 'break ranks' and come about him. In simple language, he told us who we were and what we should do and how to achieve it. His voice cleared the Mersey and I was certain that the dockers in Birkenhead thought he was getting at them!

In 1981 the Mersey Division was converted to mine-hunting and a number of vessels were attached to the Division. It also became over the years the administrative centre for the R.N.R. in the North-West and served a number of major towns and cities including Preston, Manchester, Coventry and Sheffield.

One of the privileges of being the R.N.R. Chaplain is that, even in retirement, I am able to maintain my contact, not only with Eaglet, but with the various retired officers' associations and in particular with the Walker's Old Boys Association, the Submariners' Association, the Sea

Urchins (Eaglet's retired officers), the Fleet Air Arm Association and the Wren's Association and many other Service groups on Merseyside. We are all great at 'swinging the lamp'!

1st Earl Mountbatten of Burma
and Captain Roy Humphreys-Jones

In my book, 'A Dog Collar in the Docks', I told the story of the death of my brother Petty Officer Frank Evans, in 1940 in the submarine Thistle and how in 1965 I came across Arthur Briard, who had missed that last fatal trip because of a severe cold. My story ended with the words ... 'We never saw or heard from Arthur again.' Time has moved on and I would like to continue the tale.

In the spring of 1996 I was invited to a 'bit of a do' by the Submariners' Association held in the Hanover Hotel and was warned that I would have a surprise. It was a good evening as we ate 'babies heads' and dug our bread in the gravy. That dish was common food aboard the boats - a mixture of everything wrapped into a ball of suet! At the appropriate time I read to the company the story of my brother and Arthur Briard, and ended with the words, "We never saw or heard from Arthur again ... until tonight!" There in the corner of that pub was Arthur Briard, 76 years old with Parkinsons' Disease. We talked well.

A few months later in the August, the Parish Church of Liverpool was packed as I conducted his funeral and at last was able to tell the full story ... the story of Arthur Briard, submarine gun layer extraordinaire! Just another seafarer!

Arthur joined the training ship, Exmouth, at the age of twelve and enlisted in the Royal Navy in 1935. He became a submariner in June 1939 and luck was with him when his first boat, Triumph, survived after striking a mine in the Skagerrak in December 1939. Next came Thistle which was sunk off Norway in April with no survivors ... that head-cold had saved his life!. His next boat was Trident and for his part in the sinking of a U-boat on the 8th October 1940 he was mentioned in Despatches.

In May 1942 he was drafted to the newly built P212 (later the Sahib) which was nearing completion in Birkenhead. The navigator was Lt. Commander I.E. Fraser, V.C., D.S.C., R.D., R.N.R., Conway 1936 - 38. The boat was armed with a 3" gun and he was the Gun Layer. One night an 1,500 ton Italian troopship was observed, Sahib's gun knocked out two of her 4.7" guns and crippled the engine room before the Italian even opened fire! This was later described as one of the finest single gun actions of the war.

For his part in the sinking of U301 and several supply ships he was awarded the D.S.M. on 6th April, 1943. The Sahib carried out many other gun actions, including an attack on an Italian armed tug, towing a barge on 22nd April, 1943. In his own words, 'Out of 72 rounds fired, we scored 70 hits, 45 of them on the tug, which was so badly damaged that it was forced to beach itself and its tow'.

On 24th April, 1943, following a successful torpedo attack on a heavily escorted Italian merchant ship, the Sahib was repeatedly attacked with a total of 51 depth-charges, but managed to surface before she sank. With the rest of the crew he was placed in captivity by the Italians. Taken to Germany for interrogation, he was returned to an Italian prisoner-of-war camp, where his immediate aim was to escape (in common with many other Sahib P.O.W.s - 19 managed to escape and 14 successfully got back home).

Arthur was involved with the digging of an escape tunnel when the camp was taken over by the Germans with the intention to move all the P.O.W.s to Germany. On the morning of the camp evacuation he hid down the partly-dug tunnel, and covered up the entrance. After being concealed for a long hot day, he emerged and simply walked free out of the abandoned camp's open gate!

The next couple of months he spent fighting alongside a band of partisans until in November 1944 he walked through the German lines to the advancing Allied 5th Army and freedom. His escape received a 'Mention in Despatches' on 12th June, 1945.

After the war he remained a leading seaman until 1949 and then joined the Merchant Navy. Finally he 'swallowed the anchor' in 1973 ... a remarkable record of service. His last five voyages in the M.N. were in the Atlantic Conveyor which was later lost in the Falklands affair.

Arthur Briard was a typical seaman, completely unassuming, a quiet professional. It was a privilege to have known him.

When I retired as the R.N.R. chaplain in 1981, my successor was the Reverend John Strettle Williams. He is much loved on Merseyside. John was made a Member of the British Empire for his services as Chaplain to the Navy and the Army on Merseyside. Most families have Service connections and the Padre is always accepted by them.

In the Anglican Cathedral on the 2nd May, 1993, the Freedom of Entry into the City of Liverpool was conferred upon H.M.S. Eaglet. It was over a hundred years since Boroughs were enabled to confer the Honorary Freedom of the Borough upon the persons whom they wished to honour. The first Honorary Freeman was created in Liverpool in 1886.

At a Special Meeting of the Council held in St. George's Hall, on Wednesday the 27th day of January, 1993, in the presence of The Lord Mayor of Liverpool, Councillor Rosemary Cooper, and of a full Council it was resolved:

"That this Council, recognising the distinguished and loyal service rendered by the Royal Naval Reserve to Sovereign and Country, and noting that for over 100 years Liverpool Citizens have been recruited into the Reserve and its predecessors; wishing to declare the respect and friendship of the City and desiring this association to be fostered, do hereby confer on H.M.S. Eaglet the Freedom of Entry into the said City and the right in perpetuity on all ceremonial occasions of honouring the City by exercising the privilege of marching through the City with colours flying, drums beating and bayonets fixed."

The Anglican Cathedral Church of Christ was a wonderful setting for the Conferment of the Freedom of Entry into the City of Liverpool on May 2nd 1993. The address was given by the Ship's Chaplain, the Reverend John Williams, M.B.E., B.A., R.N.R.

"Honour.
Today's ceremony is a great honour for H.M.S. Eaglet and is valued by all members of the Ship's Company. Here, in this Cathedral Church which represents to us all something of our lives and our hopes, our aspirations and our ideals, and the Spirit of this Great City to which we belong, and on this historic day, we give thanks for the long and happy associations between the City and H.M.S. Eaglet, the inter-twined story of the generations of officers, men and women of the Mersey Division

and the citizens of this great port, the mutual support and concerns and the strengthening of one another by aiding and goodwill.

"Ideals.
Through good times and bad, through times of war and times of peace, it has been the steady maintenance of the ideals of seamanship, of patriotism and of civic pride and concern that has kept this remarkable association together, forming a bond and strength, and a flame of courage and pride.

"We give thanks for all these achievements and opportunities over a period of ninety years; we give thanks for the mutual respect and affection, care and concern between the City and Mersey Division. Here is a true family relationship, at its best, of support and care; and of encouragement towards ever better and higher service.

"Truth.
But we should beware of making this an occasion for mutual backslapping! Why? This Conferment is taking place in a Church - a very grand and magnificent Church, but still a Church - and a Church is a place of Truth. The truth is - this world is a very dangerous place.

"Bosnia is in the headlines - but that is only one place of conflict. The dangers are immense.

"Jesus did not say 'Blessed are the Peacelovers' - he said, 'Blessed are the Peacemakers!'

"And this is what we are called to be - All of us, Peacemakers. Her Majesty's Ship Eaglet exists in order to promote peace; and peacemaking is a deadly serious business.

"The Vision.
That may seem a paradox - after all do we not train for war? And is the Ship's Company not going to march through the City bearing arms? Yes, that is indeed so - because this is an imperfect world. But we must always remember Christ's words, and hold them alongside the great

vision of the Prophet Isaiah:

'They will beat their swords into ploughshares,
and their spears into pruning hooks;
nation will not lift up sword against nation,
nor ever again be trained for war.'

2.4

This can never be a safe or easy option!

"Dedication.
The Freedom of the City of Liverpool is a very gracious gesture, and is given as a sign of trust, of affection and of confidence, and we in Eaglet pray that we may be called worthy of it.

"So here in God's House, let us rededicate ourselves to training and working for peace and justice throughout God's world, that the inhabitants of our Island and Commonwealth may in peace and quietness serve the Lord our God. This is our prayer this afternoon, and this must be our constant endeavour:

Lord, when thou givest to thy servants
To endeavour in any great matter,
Grant us also to know
That it is not the beginning,
But the continuing of the same,
Until it be thoroughly finished,
That yieldeth the true glory. Amen.
Sir Francis Drake."

Such an address not only expresses the reason for the existence today of the R.N.R. and of H.M.S. Eaglet, but also explains why we must be thankful that the organisation has survived into the present century, whilst the other training ships have passed into history. In common parlance, 'For evil to prevail, let good men do nothing!'

The Duke of Edinburgh opens the new headquarters

The new home for Eaglet is alongside Harry Ramsden's Fish and Chips emporium in the South Docks. As one wag put it ... 'At least they can save a dollar or two on the galley!' The new building, 'R.N. Headquarters, Merseyside,' no longer carries the name of the old ship, and houses not only the Royal Naval Reserve, but the Royal Marines from Birkenhead and the Sea Cadets. It was formally opened by the Admiral of the Fleet, The Prince Philip, Duke of Edinburgh, KG, Kt, on the 16th October, 1998

Times ever change. Akbar, Clarence, Indefatigable and H.M.S. Conway are now memories. The work of H.M.S. Eaglet continues.

Dog Collar in the Docks

This book is much more than an autobiography. It is an encounter with almost thirty years of Ships and Seafarers in Liverpool at a time when this great port was adapting itself to the changes and challenges of the tail end of the Twentieth Century. The people are real, the pain and laughter compelling, the story is a good read. Bob Evans is part of that story. His ministry at the Mersey Mission to Seamen and the Royal Naval Reserve placed him at the forefront of waterfront life, as his 'dog collar' seems to open every door.

Mersey Mariners

The story of seafarers from the last two centuries. From sail to steam, boarding houses and crimps, extortion, poverty, the unforgiving sea; all these are vividly described. The courage of the men, the mix of nationalities and races and the cheapness of life all add colour to the scene. Against all this is the remarkable saga of the charities and welfare organisations that were set up to combat the problems. That story continues. Bob Evans is firmly part of that history and brings it alive for us in this compelling read.

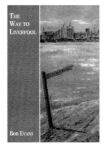

The Way to Liverpool

The basic aim was the training of young lads. H.M.S. Conway was the officers' training ship and lay a little south of Rock Ferry Pier. The Akbar, a Protestant reformatory vessel, sat between Eastham and Rock Ferry. Next in line was Indefatigable, an old sailing frigate, housing orphaned sons of seamen of good standing. Life was really tough, but the great hardships of the reformatory ships were better than the streets of Liverpool. Bob Evans is again firmly part of this history. It is the story of Liverpool seafaring.

All priced £7.00

205